W9-BLR-906

Researcher's Guide

to Archives and Regional History Sources

Researcher's

Guide

TO ARCHIVES
AND REGIONAL HISTORY SOURCES

Edited by John C. Larsen

Foreword by John Y. Cole

LIBRARY PROFESSIONAL PUBLICATIONS ▢ 1988

First published 1988 as a Library Professional Publication,
an imprint of The Shoe String Press, Inc.,
Hamden, Connecticut 06514

Printed in the United States of America

Library of Congress Cataloging in Publications Data

Researcher's guide to archives and regional history sources / edited
by John C. Larsen; foreword by John Y. Cole.

p.   cm.

Bibliography: p.

Includes index.

ISBN 0-208-02144-2 (alk. paper)

1. Archives—United States.   2. Archival materials.   3. United
States—History—Research.   4. United States—History—Archival
resources.   I. Larsen, John C., 1927–

CD3021.R47   1988

973'.072—dc19

88-15081   CIP

The paper in this publication meets the minimum
requirements of the American National Standard for
Information Sciences—Permanence of Paper for
Printed Library Materials, ANSI Z39.48-1984. ∞

CONTENTS

JOHN Y. COLE

FOREWORD

In 1970 the Librarian of Congress, L. Quincy Mumford, writing in *American Archivist*, called for increased cooperation between librarians and archivists. Acknowledging the differences between the kinds of research materials collected and the methods of organization and control used by each, Mumford nonetheless felt that the growing similarities between libraries and archives made better communication imperative. Moreover, increased cooperation would help achieve an important shared purpose: serving the researcher more effectively. In making his case, the Librarian of Congress described research performed in the Library of Congress and other large federal libraries, emphasizing how archives, historical records, and traditional library resources were increasingly being used in combination.

The interests of librarians, archivists, and historians have continued to merge since 1970. The computer and other new technologies have helped librarians and archivists cooperate to establish technical standards and formats that they can share. Preservation and issues relating to copyright and literary property, access and confidentiality, fund-raising and public relations have become recognized as common concerns. The professional associations representing librarians, archivists, and historians have begun exchanging information and developing joint projects. The closer cooperation that Librarian of Congress Mumford advocated is taking place.

Moreover, since 1970 our concept of the resources useful for research has expanded. The movement toward interdisciplinary studies, the increased interest in genealogy and popular culture, and a new historical focus on the activities of the common citizen have highlighted the usefulness of local history collections, public records, and specialized resources that have been accumulated but neglected for many years. New techniques in the collection of oral history have become much more sophisticated; the value of such history has been recognized and its popularity has grown.

But what is happening within the libraries themselves, particularly the smaller libraries that cannot approach the Library of Congress or other large research institutions in resources, collections, or staff? This *Researcher's Guide to Archives and Regional History Sources* is aimed both at researchers and at the librarians who work in such libraries. Its useful and authoritative descriptions of research techniques and archival resources will be especially helpful to librarians who are not specialists in archival or historical resources. It provides basic introductions to traditional sub-fields and to relatively new areas of concern, such as oral history and preservation. Thus it serves as a valuable "finder's aid" to the state of archival and historical research resources in the 1980s. Archives and libraries share a common purpose: to collect, maintain, and make available the written and graphic record of our civilization. This common purpose makes sense only if the resources and techniques of each are made known to an ever-increasing audience of potential users. Such is the purpose of this volume.

This *Researcher's Guide*, then, is a book of practical value. But it also can be seen as an aid and encouragement to public libraries in their vital roles as cultural institutions. I am thinking in particular of the valuable function that public libraries can perform in meeting the cultural needs of communities through alliances with local colleges, schools, historical societies, archives, and museums. Knowledge of the resources of other institutions helps librarians extend their services to diverse segments of society and to function as important bridges between scholarship and the non-academic public. Referral services to institutions that are not libraries, continuing education for out-of-school adults, and cultural programming for the entire community are logical functions for an institution that symbolizes the American democratic faith in popular education.

The alliance that joins historical research, the American public library, and the local community is a natural one. Its importance was recognized in 1980 when the Rockefeller Foundation's Commission on the Humanities, in its report, *The Humanities in Ameri-*

can Life, called the public library "the single most important cultural institution in most communities." The Commission also concluded that preserving the vitality of the public library "is unequivocally in the national interest." Books such as *Researcher's Guide to Archives and Regional History Sources* are useful to researchers, to librarians, to all of us who recognize the crucial role that libraries play in the communities they serve—and in our culture itself.

John Y. Cole
The Center for the Book
Library of Congress

PREFACE

This guide is intended to help the researcher whose work requires the use of archival records, for resources which go beyond printed library materials. The guide provides a background for archival research, identifying basic procedures and tools, and suggesting ways in which research can be undertaken efficiently.

Archival materials are unique. If an archival document is lost or damaged, it cannot be replaced in the way that a lost copy of a recent best-seller can. Because of the irreplaceability and individuality of archival materials, the researcher will find that, in general, there are restrictions on using them, resulting not from any unwillingness to make information available, but from the fragility and rarity of the items.

Each chapter of this guide has been written by an experienced archivist with expertise in the chapter's topic. The authors, who represent a variety of institutions throughout the United States, are aware that every archives differs in material and rules of operation. The beginning researcher is urged to discuss his or her research project in detail with the archives staff; an archival collection may contain information not immediately apparent to a researcher unfamiliar with the collection and local finding aids, and the staff may know of relevant material in another institution which has never been cited in catalogs and bibliographies.

THE CONTRIBUTORS

WILLA K. BAUM, director of the Regional Oral History Office at the University of California at Berkeley, is the author of *Oral History for the Local Historical Society* and *Transcribing and Editing Oral History*. A frequent speaker at professional meetings and training workshops, Mrs. Baum has served on the Oral History Association council and the Society of American Archivists oral history committee.

BONNIE JO CULLISON is preservation librarian and head of the Conservation Department at the Newberry Library in Chicago. An active member of the Chicago Area Conservation Group and an officer of the Chicago Hand Bookbinders, she has published articles describing the Newberry Library's environmentally controlled bookstack building.

CHRISTOPHER DENSMORE, associate archivist in the University Archives at the State University of New York at Buffalo, is a regular contributor to professional journals. His special research interests include archival arrangement and description and Quaker bibliography. He is currently chair of the Description Section of the Society of American Archivists.

ROMAN DRAZNIOWSKY, curator of the American Geographical Society Collection, is the author of *Map Librarianship: Readings* and *Cataloging and Filing Rules for Maps and Atlases,* as well as many articles on cartography and related subjects. Professor of library science at the University of Wisconsin-Milwaukee, Dr. Drazniowsky is the editor of *Current Geographical Publications.*

DAVID B. GRACY II, Governor Bill Daniel Professor in Archival Enterprise at the University of Texas at Austin, was formerly director of the Texas State Archives. A past president of the Society of American Archivists, Dr. Gracy has written extensively on archives; his works include *Archives and Manuscripts: Arrangement and Description* and *An Introduction to Archives and Management.*

BONNIE HARDWICK is head of the Manuscripts Division of the Bancroft Library at the University of California at Berkeley. Dr. Hardwick was formerly manuscripts specialist in the Western History Department of the Denver Public Library.

OTTILIA KOEL is librarian and curator of manuscripts at the Whitney Library of the New Haven Colony Historical Society in Connecticut. Mrs. Koel has been active in the History Section of the American Library Association, the Society of American Archivists, the New England Archivists, the Local History and Genealogy Division of the Connecticut Library Association, and the Connecticut League of Historical Societies, and she has conducted workshops for archivists.

PHILIP F. MOONEY is the manager of the Archives Department of the Coca-Cola Company in Atlanta. Currently chair of the Business Archives Section of the Society of American Archivists, Mr. Mooney conducts annual workshops on business archives for the Society and is a regular contributor to professional journals.

JUDITH ANN SCHIFF, chief research archivist in the Manuscripts and Archives Department of the Yale University Library, has published articles on Yale University, New Haven, and Charles A. Lindbergh. Ms. Schiff has conducted workshops and lectured at archivists' meetings on family history and the importance of artifacts and photographs in manuscript collections.

FLOYD M. SHUMWAY, recently retired executive director of the New Haven Colony Historical Society in Connecticut, has taught at Columbia University, New York University, and Yale University. Dr. Shumway currently serves on the boards of the Committee for a New England Bibliography, the Connecticut Coordinat-

ing Committee for the Promotion of History, and the Friends of
the New Haven Public Library

MARGARET F. STIEG is professor of library service at the University of Alabama Graduate School of Library Service. Her principal
areas of research are scholarly communication and library history.
She recently published *The Origin and Development of Scholarly
Historical Periodicals* and is at present working on a book about
public libraries under the Nazis. The recipient of research grants
from the Council on Library Resources and the German Academic
Exchange Service, Dr. Stieg is also active in professional associations, and serves currently on the board of editors of the *Journal of
Education for Library and Information Science.*

ENID T. THOMPSON, former head of the Colorado Historical
Society Library and director of archival studies at the University of
Denver, has recently completed research and archival assignments
for the U.S. Bureau of Mines, the American Academy of Religion,
the Society of Biblical Literature, and Regis College in Denver.

MARGARET F. STIEG

1. INTRODUCTION
TO ARCHIVAL RESEARCH

Historical research is a complex process that begins with framing questions, goes on to collecting information, progresses to analysis, and ends with presentation of the results. At its heart are archives. Almost invariably, the search for information will take the researcher to an agency, archival or otherwise, that collects historical documents. This chapter will tell the beginning researcher in an archival collection what to expect and how to use the collection effectively.

Archives, manuscript libraries, records centers, and regional history collections preserve our heritage and serve as a collective memory. Research libraries also participate to some extent in this enterprise. Although these institutions specialize in somewhat different aspects of these purposes, they share one common concern: the preservation of original source materials that document the past. They collect, organize, describe, and make accessible much that would otherwise be lost or available only to a privileged few.

The growth of archives parallels the rise of the modern historical profession. In the nineteenth century, telling the story "as it really happened"[1] became the standard of historical scholarship; to find out what "really happened," it was necessary to go to original sources. Modern historical scholarship is inseparable from documentary research.

In the early days, the historian was often a collector. The renowned Bancroft Library of the University of California owes its existence to one such private enterprise. To write his histories of California and the other Pacific states, Hubert Howe Bancroft brought together the largest and most complete collection of original historical material on the western half of North America. Bancroft sent copyists to California's provincial archives, to the

1

mission archives, and to the land office. He persuaded old-time settlers to dictate their experiences, a pioneer venture in oral history. He amassed thousands of volumes of local newspapers. Eventually, this unparalleled resource was purchased by the University of California.[2]

Twentieth-century researchers can take advantage of a network of well-established archives and manuscript repositories. The first state archives was that of Alabama, created in 1901; the National Archives was finally established under President Franklin D. Roosevelt after a long campaign that brought together archivists, historians, and patriotic groups.[3] In addition to archives and records centers that serve federal, state, and municipal governments, archives are maintained by corporations, churches, and other organizations. There are many private historical societies, like the New-York Historical Society, whose collections have a very specific focus, such as the Irish experience in America or aviation history. Others, like the American Antiquarian Society, have few restrictions of time, place, or subject. Research libraries with manuscripts divisions may also specialize, as does the Newberry Library in American and English history; or, like Harvard, their area of interest may be so broad that their collections include historical materials on subjects from many places and time periods.

All of these organizations provide the raw material for history: original sources. In the nineteenth century, "original source" meant written documents; today, archival and manuscript collections contain documentation in any form in which information is available, encompassing film, recordings, and machine readable data, as well as manuscripts. To shed light on societies and topics for which written records are scanty or nonexistent, archives have begun to collect a wide variety of nontraditional materials, such as aerial photographs, artifacts, and oral histories. The subjects represented in collections reflect the diversity of current historical inquiry which extends far beyond the nineteenth-century emphasis on European and American political history, to include social and economic questions, new geographic areas, and such formerly neglected groups as blacks and women.

In their use of source material, regardless of its subject or physical format, modern historians make a fundamental distinction between primary and secondary source materials. A *primary source* is one created by a witness to or the first recorder of an event, often a participant. This type of source permits the researcher to approach an event more closely and directly than in any other way. Examples of primary sources are the diaries of Count Ciano, Mussolini's son-in-law and foreign minister, or the Watergate tapes. So are the innumerable reports, memoranda, and letters generated by institutions and individuals while carrying out their daily business. *Primary source* usually, but not invariably, means unpublished material; for a study of political opinion in the Midwest, editorials published in local newspapers might be an appropriate primary source. Drawing on first-hand reports, historians produce *secondary* accounts which digest and interpret the evidence. Texts and syntheses in turn draw upon the literature that is the result of archival research to address a less specialized audience.

The relationship between primary and secondary accounts can be graphically presented (see fig. 1). An event takes place; it has a reality that time does not change. Human memory being what it is, firsthand accounts produced at or near the time of the event are likely to recount the event more accurately than those produced after significant time has passed. (We will leave the question of how to interpret evidence until later.) Historians use primary sources, selecting information to suit their purposes. How closely their accounts approach the reality of the event depends on how informative their sources are and on their ability to interpret them and

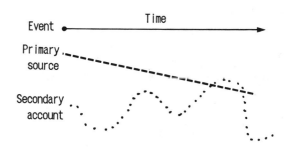

FIG. 1. The relationship between primary and secondary accounts.

choose the most relevant evidence. They can never recreate the event with total accuracy.

Source materials have several different kinds of values; perhaps the simplest is their intrinsic value as an object or artifact. Some manuscripts and photographs are works of art in their own right, and individuals and institutions acquire them for aesthetic considerations. One can appreciate an illuminated Arabic manuscript even if one reads no Arabic. That kind of appreciation, however, is far different from the kind a historian would have for a letter by Ronald Reagan explaining his reasons for bombing Libya, or a genealogist for a great-grandfather's long-sought will.

Another kind of value is associational. To have contact with something that a famous individual owned or used can be very moving; at the very least it brings that person closer and makes the past more real. That is why institutions will preserve the cup from which Charles II drank during his escape after the Battle of Worcester, George Washington's false teeth, and the scarf that strangled Isadora Duncan. The associational value is one reason why every scrap of paper written by Thomas Jefferson or Benjamin Franklin is prized. Even the most blasé scholar feels excitement when, in the occasionally tedious course of research on some worthy topic, a volume of sixteenth- and seventeenth-century manuscript letters is discovered to contain one written by Queen Elizabeth. That letter, in her spiky, distinctive and rather beautiful handwriting, can be read, touched, and absorbed, at least as appreciatively as the letters by the little-known Dean of Wells, which were the topic of research that led to the discovery.

Artifactual and associational values are concepts that derive from our culture, but, while they may make research more exciting, they are largely incidental. Archivists and manuscript curators decide what to preserve on the basis of informational value. The vast majority of users seek out manuscripts because of their content.

Manuscripts and other historical sources contain information that is not available elsewhere. Often it is unique. To read John Cole's testimony about the radical itinerant minister who visited the village of Chew Magna in 1640, one must travel to the Somerset Record Office in Taunton, England, where the records of the diocese of Bath and Wells are held. Only by going to the baptismal register of St. Francis Episcopal Church, the military records in the National Archives, and the wills in the Tuscaloosa County courthouse can the bare facts of Grandpa Snazzy's life be reconstructed. Modern office technology and changing bureaucratic practices have greatly reduced the number of documents that are physically unique and the amount of information that is substantively unique, but carbon paper, photocopying, and a universal practice of generating voluminous reports have changed the nature of research less than earlier historians anticipated. From the researcher's point of view, it still makes sense to visit an archive or collection with a high concentration of memoranda or reports that, while not unique, are otherwise widely scattered. Just because a document began life as one of a printing of one hundred, it does not mean that all one hundred copies of it survived. Archivists and collectors know that some of the material that is most difficult to find after time has passed is material that was very abundant when it was created, such as leaflets handed out at rallies, posters used to announce an event, or handbooks distributed to an organization's entire membership.

Despite gaps and absences in collections, a massive quantity of material is the hallmark of modern historical research, although abundance varies depending on locale and time period. Generally speaking, the closer the incident or subject is to the present, the greater the amplitude. Historians of the United States are better off than European historians and much better off than African historians, thanks to such historical accidents as a comparatively recent start, a well-developed historical consciousness among its founders, and a beneficent climate. This pattern is, however, painted in broad brush strokes only, and there are many individual anomalies. Although some sensitive material is deliberately destroyed, similar documents often survive because a participant hopes to vindicate himself in a particular situation. It is, for example, difficult to study the development of the historical profession because relatively few collections of the personal papers of historians are left. And if historians themselves fail to appreciate the significance of documents, it is vain to expect greater historical consciousness from others. Fire, water, and war have wrought serious damage on the documentary record. In an English example of one of life's ironies, the Somerset wills—which had been sent for safekeeping during

World War II from Taunton, an important railway junction, to Exeter, a quiet cathedral town—were destroyed in a bombing of Exeter, while archives remaining in Taunton survived.

The volume of records of all kinds has increased dramatically since the beginning of the nineteenth century. To meet the steadily expanding responsibilities of governments, bureaucracies grew; in the United States of 1816 there were 4,837 civilian employees of the national government. In 1984 there were 2,824,000.[4] Records are, as Max Weber remarked, the bureaucrat's tools of production. The profusion was intensified by the revolution in office technology. Typewriter, stenotype machine, dictaphone, mimeograph, and, ultimately, the photocopier all made it easier to produce more, if not better, information. Private papers have grown correspondingly. In the nineteenth century the spread of education in Europe and America produced more people who were able to record their activities and correspond with one another. A simultaneous improvement in living conditions provided societies with the leisure for activity beyond that necessary to insure physical and spiritual survival.

Abundant source materials are a mixed blessing. Thoroughness is an axiom of good scholarship, but where does one draw the line? If a student of a particular event has used the records of the Department of State and the Department of Defense but ignored those of the Treasury Department, that failure may prevent publication of the research or, if it is published, elicit a poor review from a scholar familiar with the unused collection who can point out important missing information or lost insights. On the other hand, the too-thorough scholar dies unpublished.

A quantity of research material requires systematic work habits. References must be thorough and exact. Notes must be organized, perhaps even indexed. A large-scale project may justify the investment of time and money for learning to use relevant computer software, such as a statistical package or an indexing program.

Abundant source material also means that vital information often lies unknown in an archival collection, waiting to be uncovered and appreciated. A routine report from the Bridgewater chief of police in the recently opened files of the Massachusetts State Police offers concrete evidence that the prosecution in the famous Sacco-Vanzetti case knowingly sent Vanzetti to the electric chair on false evidence.[5]

The pack rat habits of Erwin Ackerknecht, a leader in the German public library profession in the first half of the century, and his success in transporting his papers from Stettin, across war-torn Germany to a safe place near Stuttgart, preserved a most interesting letter about Nazi antilibrary activities before 1933. That letter, buried among tailor's receipts, form thank-you letters, and innumerable drafts of publications, provided the indispensable clue to locating significant documentation in a city now located in East Germany.

Some primary sources of the highest interest have been put into print, such as the papers of the presidents of the United States or the documents in *Foreign Relations of the United States*.[6] Often read by nonscholars with a serious interest in their nation's history, these compilations contribute to an informed citizenry. Although they make available material wanted by many historians and help researchers in preliminary planning, they are no substitute for a personal visit to the archives. Printed sources encompass only a tiny fraction of the relevant material and, when sources have been printed, they may not be reliable.

The successive editions of the writings of George Washington demonstrate how standards of historical editing have changed as historical scholarship has evolved. Between 1834 and 1837, Jared Sparks, a former editor of the *North American Review*, published the first edition of Washington's writings. To adjust Washington's eighteenth-century attitudes and vocabulary to Victorian sensibilities, Sparks made liberal changes. "Dirty" was omitted from a description of the "dirty mercenary spirit" of the Connecticut troops, "Old Put" emerged as "General Putnam," and the statement that a certain sum "will be but a fleabite to our demands" became "will be totally inadequate." Sharp criticism of Sparks's practices by Lord Mahon and John Bigelow contributed to the acceptance of literal accuracy as the rule for historical editing. Since then Washington's writings have been reedited by Worthington C. Ford (1889–93), who was highly critical of Sparks, and then by John C. Fitzpatrick (1931–44), whose work often corrects that of Ford.[7]

Editors have the obligation both to reproduce texts faithfully and to make them intelligible. The relative balance they strike between these sometimes conflicting ideals depends upon who the prospective reader is conceived to be. It makes sense to reproduce faithfully every archaic spelling and every capital letter of the diaries of John Harington, a relatively unknown mid-seventeenth-century English lawyer and member of Parliament. His diaries do not make easy reading, but probably no one without a serious and professional interest in seventeenth-century England is likely to read them. Editors of texts with more popular appeal, or those editors with a responsibility to a wider public, like the editors of the papers of Thomas Jefferson or the Adams family, make different choices.[8]

Another kind of problem printed sources can present is illustrated by the *Calendar of Letters and Papers of Henry VIII.*[9] Archivists emphasize the importance of *respect des fonds* (original order) and provenance because the source of a document or group of documents, and the original order of the documents, can reveal a great deal in and of themselves. After their attempt to locate all of Henry VIII's writings, the compilers of the *Calendar* arranged them chronologically, destroying the original order and giving a misleading impression of completeness. When the British Public Record Office decided to bind its share of Henry's letters and papers (which were the bulk of the documents) in the order of the *Calendar,* important evidence was lost forever.[10] There are, therefore, many reasons for the conscientious researcher or eager family historian to seek out original manuscripts. Fortunately, research can also be fun. It can, in fact, be so much fun that it becomes an end in itself. Barbara Tuchman, author of *The Guns of August,* suggests a solution adapted from advice given to her by her mother on the subject of dating: always leave a half hour before you want to. It is sound advice. Tuchman tells of the woman she met while she was looking for documents on Pericardis, an American captured by Moroccan brigands in 1904. This woman had been doing research on relations between the United States and Morocco since writing her dissertation in 1936. When Tuchman met her, she was in her seventies and had recently suffered a heart attack.[11] Any scholar or archivist can match this cautionary tale. There are biographies of Melvil Dewey (of Dewey decimal classification fame), and of Richard Henry Lee (a signer of the Declaration of Independence), lying unwritten and unpublished because the author has allowed research to become an end in itself, just as monographs on colonial piracy and Prussian administration, studies of Texas politics and French syndicalism, and the genealogy of more than one family have never seen the light of day.

The late nineteenth century was the heroic age of manuscript research. Historians knew that they needed documents, but European countries were only beginning to create the archives and develop the policies that would make it possible for researchers to use government records. Sometimes researchers had to take the initiative in persuading governments to open their files. Henry Adams's letters to James Russell Lowell paint an interesting picture of research at this time. To tell the "whole truth" in his *History of the United States from 1801 to 1815* Adams wanted to consult relevant European documents. The British government had to change its rules to allow him to see its records, a feat undoubtedly facilitated by his family connections. The "gift" of a gown from his wife to the wife of a minor official unlocked the archives of Seville for him. [12]

The historians of the nineteenth century were pioneers. To them belonged the satisfaction of being first to use the governmental records of the major European powers. Mining sources of such high interest was gratifying work, and the discovery of a particularly rich lode might deflect a historian from his original plans, as the Venetian archives did Leopold von Ranke. His book, *The Ottoman and Spanish Empires in the Sixteenth and Seventeenth Centuries,* took advantage of the detailed reports of the Venetian ambassadors which he was the first to use. [13]

Not all the excitement vanished with the turn of the century. Ulrich B. Phillips, the Southern historian, can take much credit for finding, preserving, and using the archival and manuscript materials of the South. As a young graduate student, C. Vann Woodward recognized the value of the Populist Tom Watson's papers and realized that a book written from them would address the central themes of Southern history and expose the fallacies of the New South school of historians. Even today, important materials will surface about even the most well studied events. Professor Leo Hershkowitz found the New York City accounting records of the Tweed era while working on the finances of the Colonial period. [14]

Preliminary planning is crucial to the final success of a project. The valedictory of the unfortunate Mary Stuart, "In my ending is my beginning," contains a profound truth for the researcher. For the historical researcher, planning begins with selecting a topic, and the wise scholar keeps in mind the availability of source material that can provide evidence. It is possible either to frame a question and then look for sources, or to find a rich source and then develop worthwhile questions that can be answered from it. Thanks to the abundance of documentation, American historians usually have the luxury of proceeding in the first manner. Others are not so fortunate.

After the topic is chosen, the next step is determining what kinds of records should be consulted. Wide background reading in secondary sources can clarify the outlines of the chosen topic and suggest a particular perspective from which it may be viewed or indicate gaps in knowledge. To locate records, the most comprehensive printed guides, such as the *National Union Catalog of Manuscript Collections,* are consulted; if the topic is a specialized one, appropriate specialized guides such as *Women's History Sources, A Guide to Archives and Manuscript Collections in the United States* are used. (See chapter 5.) After repositories have been identified, their catalogs should be searched, and finding aids to individual collections should then be used. Most finding aids are only available at the repository itself; the calendar series of the Public Record Office is a rare exception.

This systematic, step-by-step approach works well, but it assumes that the necessary printed guides exist. What does a researcher do if they do not? The planning and advance work done for a project in modern German history illustrates what may be required.

The role of public libraries under the Nazis was a topic that grew out of earlier research. When investigation uncovered no previous research either in German or English, the search for source material began. There are only a few printed guides to German archives and manuscript collections. These were consulted, with very little result. Letters to the national archives in both East and West Germany confirmed that the records of the two organizations in the national government responsible for public libraries had been destroyed, burned in Allied bombing of Berlin in late 1944. The next step was to contact the provincial archives. Once materials relating to public libraries were found in provincial archives, the larger cities in the province were then contacted in search of records that would complement those at the provincial level. Abundant records of provincial library administrations made the study possible, and eventually they became the core of the evidence.

Because the Nazi period is relatively recent, it was possible to supplement documentary evidence with interviews. A letter to the Deutsches Bibliotheksinstitut produced a list of important public librarians active during the Nazi period who were still alive. When the researcher arrived in Germany, archivists and the former librarians suggested additional sources, including people and materials. One such contact had helped to organize a campaign to persuade the director of the German national library organization not to resign and had copies of his letters to the director. No mention of this campaign had been discovered in any of the dozens of collections used. Generally, however, interviews are more useful for what they offer on perspective and feelings than on specific facts.

Family historians and genealogists proceed somewhat differently, both because their subjects are determined for them and because they are after a single, isolated fact rather than more comprehensive information. For them creativity consists of figuring out where to go to corroborate a fact, rather than conceptualizing a problem. Genealogical research is a special kind of detective work; the genealogist begins with an assumption or probability and then seeks proof. Verifying one assumption may reveal new clues, to be confirmed in their turn, until the complete family line is established. The genealogist's task is both easier and more difficult than that of other researchers; easier because his choices are imposed upon him, more difficult because predetermination precludes pursuing a somewhat different topic if the original choice does not work out.

A good example of genealogical research is Alex Haley's search for his ancestors. It provided the raw material for both the book and the television program *Roots*. Haley began with a family tradition that spoke of a slave ancestor, "the African," who called a guitar "ko," and his childhood river "Kamby Balongo." To reconstruct his family tree, Haley used census listings, maritime documents, old newspapers, and courthouse records. He consulted an expert on African linguistics. Eventually he arrived in the Gambian village of Juffure where a *griot*, a tribal oral historian, was able to provide the final link to his African heritage with the story of Kunta Kinte, who at the age of seventeen went out one day to chop wood and was never seen again.[15]

In pursuing the family tree, novice researchers need to familiarize themsleves with the kinds of records in which birth and death dates, names of children and parents, occupations and addresses are listed. They are likely to use many archives and manuscript collections rather than just a few. Numerous printed sources designed for this research, such as name indexes to collections of wills, are available, and special collections, such as the Local History and Genealogy Collection at the New York Public Library, cater to their needs.

Whether the researcher is a historian, genealogist, lawyer, or curious citizen, locating source material is only the first stage of research. Sometimes gaining access may be a problem. There are few things more frustrating than knowing that needed information exists but lies out of reach. Government records may be closed for a certain period of time after an event; Britain, for example, has a thirty-year rule. Private papers may be given to an institution with similar time restrictions to protect survivors. Families and other bodies sensitive about their reputations, or lacking the necessary facilities, may refuse to open their records to outsiders. In Germany laws to protect individual privacy have created additional obstacles. In the Soviet Union access appears to be governed by pure caprice.

After the scholar actually has the long-sought sources in hand, they must be read and understood, a process that is not quite as clear-cut as it may seem. The typewriter did not come into general use until the end of the nineteenth century and even today many records, especially personal ones, are not typed. Handwritten documents present numerous problems. When the writer of a document was a professional scribe or clerk, the record usually is not especially difficult to read, if the researcher has mastered the conventions of the period. That is, however, a fairly challenging "if." For example, medieval scripts employ numerous abbreviations. A bar over a series of letters denotes an unspecified number of upright strokes left out. The letters of the alphabet constructed solely of varying numbers of these strokes include m, n, i, j, and u. The word "minimum" might be written with three or four strokes and a bar over them; it was the reader's responsibility to decode the result by providing the correct number of upright strokes. Many of these originally Latin abbreviations continued to be used into the seventeenth century, in both English and Latin documents.

Handwriting based on Gothic letters continued in use for special purposes, such as legal documents, but during the Renaissance an Italian writing style known variously as Italic, chancery, or secretary hand, came into general use over Europe. A cursive handwriting with rounded letter forms, it was the writing of the Elizabethans and, with a little practice, is not difficult for twentieth-century Americans to read. Copperplate, which replaced it, is even easier because our schools still teach a modified version of copperplate. Only Russian and German handwriting is significantly different, the former because it derived from the completely different Cyrillic alphabet, the latter because Germany clung to handwriting styles derived from Gothic rather than Roman models, and neither was influenced by Italic. A nineteenth-century German handwritten lowercase *e,* for example, looks like a modern *n,* a lower case *h,* like an *f.*

Fortunately for the researcher who needs to read handwritten documents, there is help. Paleography, the study of ancient handwriting, is a discipline in its own right, and there are useful manuals available. Modern handwriting has not attracted such scholarly attention, but contemporary handwriting manuals are more than adequate compensation. Just like the handwriting guides used in elementary schools today, they were designed to teach individuals to write and can be used by researchers who wish to learn to read nineteenth-century German script or understand the meaning of a no-longer-used eighteenth-century feature.[16]

A talent for crossword puzzles is a great asset in reading handwritten documents. The same vocabulary skills and willingness to try different letters is required, and the researcher has the bonus of a context to help. Nothing, however, is of much avail when handwriting is bad. Bad handwriting is bad handwriting, whether it is that of a twentieth-century high school student or a seventeenth-century lawyer. Carelessly formed letters, incomplete strokes, and crowding will always cause problems. The difficulty is compounded when the writer in question either cannot spell or was writing in an era before spelling was standardized and dictionaries were widely used.

While gathering evidence, the researcher must be thorough. Barbara Tuchman cites a telling example when persistence paid off handsomely. For her biography of General Stilwell, she was reading the newspaper of the regiment to which he was attached in China from 1926 to 1929. She had luckily found a full run on microfilm at the New York Public Library. A laborious scan of every page on the first reel yielded nothing of interest. Ready to give up, her conscience forced her to look at the second reel. On the first page of the first issue was an article by Stilwell, the first of a series on the personalities and issues of the Chinese civil war. This series gave Tuchman what every historian dreams of, the views of her subject on critical events at the time they were taking place.[17]

After sources have been read, evaluated, and digested, researchers need to make appropriate records for their files. Handbooks for history students[18] offer basic advice on practical details (for example, take notes on only one side of the page and always identify the source of the information completely), but no book can tell the researcher *what* is important to record for later use. That is determined by the subject under examination and the questions the researcher is trying to answer.

Allan Nevins has described historical writing as consisting of three elements: factual inquiry and sifting, interpretation, and presentation.[19] The three are interrelated, and all have a bearing upon research in the archives or manuscript collection. Inquiry, sifting, and weighing are intrinsic to research; without such processing the would-be researcher in the archives is nothing but an industrious drone, accumulating facts.

Researchers must understand what they find in source material. Acquiring an educated intelligence, the experience to comprehend human behavior, mastery over facts, and depth of learning all take time. The brilliant flash of insight is always welcome, but the complexity and interrelatedness of historical materials requires a different kind of thoughtfulness as well. It is no coincidence that historians tend to improve with age.

The question "what does this mean?" must always be in mind. No single piece of evidence can be evaluated in isolation. A thorough acquaintance with Jefferson's papers, for example, reveals a consistently more radical vocabulary in his letters to younger men. Dumas Malone, a leading Jefferson scholar, regarded this less as an indication that Jefferson hoped for a new revolution, than that he was trying to awaken the coming generation to its responsibilities. From this perspective, some of Jefferson's most advanced proposals appear quite different.[20] One historian interpreted a message from Lord Rockingham to Burke, "My heart is at ease," as pleasure in Gates's defeat at the battle of Saratoga. The interpretation would have been different had the researcher known that Burke had fought a duel the morning that Rockingham sent the note. Among the letters of Thomas Cromwell, the much disliked minister of Henry VIII, are what appear to be two notes from him, blackmailing the priors of monasteries he had allegedly saved from suppression. In fact, the letters are written and signed in a hand quite different from that of Cromwell or his clerks. Their presence in Cromwell's papers indicates that he discovered, and doubtless made short work of, the plot to discredit him.[21]

This kind of examination and analysis is also necessary to unmask contemporary misrepresentation and deception. Father Louis Hennepin explored the Illinois and upper Mississippi Rivers in 1680 under LaSalle's orders and published an account of that expedition in 1683. Only after LaSalle's death did he claim that he, Hennepin, had explored the Mississippi to its mouth on that occasion, well before LaSalle's achievement. In evidence, Hennepin offered a journal with numerous details, a journal that Hennepin had created by copying sentences, even whole pages, from an authentic diary kept by Father Membré, one of LaSalle's companions. Membré's diary had been printed in a book that the Jesuits suppressed. Believing all copies destroyed, Hennepin plagiarized freely, only to stand exposed when stray copies appeared. But internal evidence alone is sufficient to discredit Hennepin. Even a schoolchild would find it difficult to accept Hennepin's description of the lower Mississippi: "It is very deep and has no sandbanks, nothing interferes with navigation, and even the largest ships might sail into it without difficulty."[22]

Verification and authentication are integral to the research process. Although Jefferson's letters and Rockingham's note to Burke were not necessarily what they seemed, they were perfectly authentic. Not all documents are legitimate; some are wholly or partially forged, and fascinating tales of historical detection have been written about cheating and dubious documents.[23] Many frauds are fairly obvious. In an account of expenses for the year 1595 found in the Trevelyan papers at the Somerset Record Office is a list of purchased books which includes *Robin Goodfellow,* Hamblett's historie, an herball, and other books. J. Payne Collier used this as evidence that the history of Hamlet upon which Shakespeare based his play was in print by 1595, a good thirteen years before the first edition of the Shakespearean play. In fact, Collier himself forged the entries, and it does not require a particularly expert eye to detect the different color of the ink and the slight variations in the shape of the letters. The four lines of forged entries were inserted in space left on the page between two lists.[24]

Fortunately, only the most important figures and the most controversial events generate enough interest to attract the forger. Interested though his great-great granddaughter may be in Grandpa Snazzy, it is extremely unlikely that anyone went to the trouble to forge a death certificate and insert it in the courthouse files. Anything as exciting as newly discovered letters of Lincoln will immediately be subjected to close scrutiny by experts. The supposed Hitler diary that made headlines in 1983 was easily discredited.

Archivists and manuscript curators are very concerned with the integrity of their records. Provenance, the origin and subsequent custody of documents, is a paramount consideration to archivists matched only by vigilance once the material is in their care. Although this attention does not solve the problem of the government official who knowingly falsified the facts in an 1872 report, or the devoted son who created or destroyed evidence to alter his father's reputation, it does prevent after-the-fact contamination.

The final stage in research, the culmination of previous activity, is presentation of results. Because what can be presented is determined by decisions made during research, the researcher dare not lose sight of the final result during the research stage becoming bogged down in detail. This is not to say that a researcher starts out to prove a case one way or another. The historian is not an advocate, and a mind closed to inconvenient evidence misses the truth. While collecting information, however, the researcher must continuously ask where it fits into the total picture. As patterns begin to emerge, it may make sense to emphasize a certain line of enquiry.

Synthesis is crucial in presentation. Without constantly addressing the question "so what?, " the final product will be nothing but
a collection of undigested data, the point of which remains obscure.
To provide structure, the researcher must select. Decisions may be
agonizing when there is more material than can be used or fitted
into the discussion, but no matter how lovingly and painstakingly
the material has been amassed, choices have to be made. Essential
facts must be included and the proper balance achieved. A single
well-chosen point can convey more than endless detail. Barbara
Tuchman brings a connoisseur's appreciation to Francis Parkman's
description of seventeenth-century French courtiers, "the butterflies
of Versailles . . . facing death with careless gallantry, in their small
three-cornered hats, powdered perukes, embroidered coats, and
lace ruffles. Their valets served them with ices in the trenches,
under the cannon of besieged towns." The image of the ices in the
trenches captures the essence of the age of Louis XIV.[25]

Good historical research requires a sense of conviction and a
point of view. Interpretation and selection go hand in hand; one is
the result of the other. The writer must establish a personal
relationship with the events being recounted. Where involvement
is lacking, the result is not only dull, but it is likely to lack
structure, conviction, and proportion; what is important will not
be distinguished from what is unimportant. Barzun and Graff have
called for an experiencing mind. Their use of the gerundive under-
lines the fact that interpretation is an active process as much as a
result. At the same time, writers must be faithful to the evidence,
not distorting it to serve their own ends.

From the first glimmer of the idea to the final product, whether
it be a scholarly paper, dissertation, family tree, or legal title,
research is a formidable undertaking. People with an interest in
historical questions will sooner or later take their search to an
archives, manuscript library, records center, or regional history
collection—repositories which preserve and make available our
past. The would-be user cannot do better than to take for a motto,
"Seek and ye shall find; knock, and it shall be opened unto you."

DAVID B. GRACY II

2. What Every Researcher Should Know about Archives

Archives are the product of a great deal of work. Therein lies their value to the researcher, as well as the requirements for their organization and retrieval. The term *Archives* is commonly used in addition to refer to both the building in which the records are housed and the administrative unit that gathers, preserves, and makes available the records. Usually *archives* employs a plural verb when used to mean *records,* while in its other meanings it commands a singular verb.

Archives are organic bodies of documentation that arise directly and naturally out of the activity of an entity, either an organization (a government, private firm, or club) or an individual. The nature of these activities, whether special or routine, occasional or daily, is unimportant. They can include conducting a business, writing bread-and-butter letters, pursuing a legal remedy in court, or preparing a reminiscence. What is crucial is that the activity, be it work or play, is performed by the entity that created and is documented by the records. The papers of John Jones, the records of the Acme Supply Company, and the records of the United States government all share this basic attribute. Each represents nothing more—and nothing less—than the documentary record of the person or organization whose archives they are. Archives are not just any records, but only those in which relationship to the creator and to each other (by virtue of their relationship to their creator) is still clear, or at least salvageable. Produced to facilitate and document the activities of their creator, archives are at the same time the record of these activities. Transition of the records to archival status occurs at an indeterminate juncture at which their role as record outweighs their role as facilitator.

The basic unit of archives is not individual letters, diaries, deeds, ledgers, photographs, or other single records, but rather a group of items (usually called a record group) formed around and recording the life and work of their creator. The group relationship of the individual documents within the archives establishes a context that the archivist uses in arranging the records and the researcher uses in interpreting the data in the records. Indeed, the authenticity of the relationship of a body of records to the person or organization that created them, which archivists make every effort to maintain and document, gives the researcher the most important context possible for understanding the information recorded.

As documentation, archives are more than records, i.e., more than the medium upon which data is recorded. Archives record the activity of people of great as well as little public importance and events both well known and obscure. Archives are maintained to hold information that the creator or researchers want to remember and use, whether for fun, profit, security, curiosity, obligation, or sentiment. However, information is worthwhile only when it is used, not merely accumulated. The accessibility of information in a body of records is no haphazard result of the survival of the material. On the contrary, the organization (arrangement) and accessibility (description) of the records reflect principles of archival enterprise that have evolved and developed over the past two hundred years. Records which are not purposefully arranged, described, and made available for use are not archives at all, but merely old records.

Modern archival enterprise is based upon three fundamental facts: archives come into being as a natural part of the process of life; they are created and treated as groups of documents; and they are maintained for the information they contain. Although they are now axiomatic to archivists at the close of the twentieth century, these three principles came only slowly into focus over a period of years. The oldest of them, that archives are treated as groups of documents, emerged at the time of the French Revolution and the founding of the Archives Nationales, the first national and the first modern archives. In strong reaction to the monarchy, the French government in the mid-1790s gathered into a central administration the records of the various ministries, which had previously been withheld from public scrutiny, and opened them to inspection by all citizens, a development without precedent. (Records of the feudal order were excepted; these were destroyed in quantity to prevent the possibility of a return to the old system.) There was no model to follow since archives formerly had only been kept, but not actively administered; there was no cadre of archivists from which the government could staff the new administration. Consequently the task fell to historians, who at least had familiarity with outdated records. The historians did what they knew how to do; they organized the records by subjects of contemporary study: the church, social development, military affairs, land tenure, and the like. The system worked well enough for the records of the *ancien régime,* which were treated as a body of closed files recording a defunct organization. However, when the records of the new government reached the Archives Nationales and received similar treatment, the government often found that it had lost touch with its memory, since agencies were unable to refer readily to their own records. Subsequently, in 1841, the archivists of France adopted the principle of *respect des fonds,* keeping the records of each agency together in groups and not intermingling them with records of other offices. Within each group they continued to arrange the records by subjects of historical inquiry and interest.

Thus the French took the first step toward recognition of the fact that records represent the work out of which they arose, but the next step was taken by the Prussians. For forty years, the archivists responsible for the diplomatic records in the Prussian Privy State Archives in Berlin followed the French lead, but instead of arranging the records by broad subjects representing fields of study, the Prussians divided their diplomatic records by the names of countries. Although names and boundaries of countries changed dramatically over the years, the filing pattern of the archives remained static. By the early 1880s, the Prussian archivists had to perform mental gymnastics to fit records representing the political geography of their day into a filing system reflecting the scheme of a half-century earlier. In 1885 the Prussian archivists abandoned the old system for one adaptable to any situation. Records were thereafter maintained in groups by the office of creation and arranged in the other in which the records were created, filed, and used by that office. This "principle of provenance," as it has become known, holds that records are more readily found and used the more accurately they follow the filing pattern of the creator. Records should not only represent the work of the creator, through being grouped by the creating entity, but should reflect the order of that work faithfully through preservation of the sequence in which the records were produced.

In reflecting the work of the generating entity, archives can be regarded as the records of yesterday's today. Archives originate as records produced to facilitate the work of the creating entity on the day they were created. Records containing information of continuing value, documenting its creator and appropriate for archival preservation, continue to be created every day. When do records become archives? The distinguishing feature of archives is not age alone. Archives are records that have exchanged short-term, regular, immediate use by the creator for long-term, less regular, but no less immediate use by users of all kinds (including the creator) for purposes beyond those for which the records were created. Theodore R. Schellenberg, the archival theorizer and popularizer, has called these two uses the "first life" and "second life" of records.[1] Because some activities require more time for completion than others, no one can draw a line across the history of any contemporary creator of records and state categorically that all older records on one side are automatically archives, while newer records on the other side are not. The line separating records that are archives from records on their way to becoming archives is a relative one, drawn on the basis of the need for the record in conducting the business for which it was created.

Archives cannot be defined by type of document any more than they can by age. The media formats of the documentary records that compose a record group can be as broad and varied as the information they record. Archivists recognize ten generic types of documentation, reflecting activity represented and purpose served: diaries, minutes, and proceedings; financial documents; legal documents; photographic material; graphic documents, including maps, charts, and graphs; scrapbooks and scrapbook material; printed material; literary productions, including oral history; and machine-readable records. Machine-readable records are both a type of material and a medium for holding information. Other media include paper, parchment, photographic negatives and prints, motion picture film, and microforms.

Archivists call the entity that creates and is in turn documented by archives a "creator." The typical creator personally produces only a portion of the records in the creator's archives. While the core of most archives is formed around outgoing letters, diaries, a variety of financial and legal records, and perhaps a selection of other documentation written by the creator, a second and usually substantial portion is composed of letters and other documents relating to the creator and obtained directly from *their* various creators. A third portion (newspaper clippings, flyers, and other printed material) has to be gathered. Although some records, such as diaries and reminiscences of individuals or minutes and memoranda of organizations, are produced especially to document the creator, the majority are not. Letters, for example, are written primarily to convey information to the addressee and only secondarily, if at all, to document action of the creator. In essence, archives are generated as an administrative function of their creator.

Appreciating this basic characteristic of archives is fundamental to conducting effective research. Archives are not subject files made up from letters, photographs, diaries, receipts, depositions, and other records for the purpose of facilitating historical, legal, genealogical, or any other kind or field of research. Many collections of individual documents gathered around a subject or interest, although found in archival repositories, are not archives at all. Examples would be the accumulation of love letters assembled from throughout the world at the West Vancouver (British Columbia) Public Library or the collection of signatures in the Declaration of Texas Independence Signers Collection in the Eugene C. Barker Texas History Center at the University of Texas at Austin. No entity—"love" or "Declaration of Texas Independence"—generated either group of documents. The individual items lack an administrative relationship—the hallmark of archives—to the group of which they are a part. The critical researcher draws a distinction between these *artificial collections,* as archivists term them, and *archives.* The information available to the user of the items in artificial collections is limited to that contained in the document itself. All context is lost.

To repeat for emphasis: archives are the records of a creator. More particularly, archives are "records, organically related, of an entity (individual or organization) systematically maintained, after they have fulfilled the purpose for which they were created, because they contain information of continuing value."

Traditionally, archivists have distinguished sharply between archives and historical manuscripts, defining archives narrowly as the records of the organization (a university, for example) of which the archival repository is a unit. (For a repository on a university campus, archives would include only the administrative records of the school.) *Historical manuscripts* would include everything else: all records and documents ranging from single literary productions to organic bodies of papers (archives—following the definition above—of entities other than the university) collected by the repository. The terminology reflects the approach of historical societies and libraries since state and local historical societies began collecting original records shortly after the creation of the country. For more than a century these institutions sought out items largely as historical artifacts of their creator.

Today historical manuscripts are sought primarily for the information they contain, and only secondarily for their artifactual interest. They are maintained purposely as the organic records of their creator, and are archives by our definition. The usefulness of the term *historical manuscripts* lies in the fact that it reflects the purpose for which the material is kept and the way in which it is consequently treated. Archives maintained by their creator are kept primarily for their use in administering the affairs of the creator. That explains why so few businesses open their noncurrent records to researchers. The records retain a proprietary and, to use Schellenberg's term, a *first life* value. Archives (historical manuscripts) collected by an educational institution, for example, are acquired for their research value. They are kept for their usefulness to researchers pursuing all manner of knowledge in a historical context.

Whether kept for research or administrative use, all archives possess a special informational value that most records lack. It has been estimated that less than 5 percent of the records of large organizations have archival value.

The act of appraisal, to decide which records to keep and which to discard, is a twentieth-century American innovation, a response to a pressing need during the 1930s and 1940s. At this time it became necessary to determine quickly, systematically, and accurately which of the voluminous records created by federal agencies during the Depression and World War II could be disposed of and which merited preservation to document the government in the National Archives. Inundated by requests from agencies desperate to recover space packed with outdated records, the staff of the National Archives, and Theodore Schellenberg in particular, had to develop a system for determining which records had lasting (often called "continuing," "enduring," or "historical") informational value.

Modern archival appraisers approach their duties from three separate perspectives. First, they examine the merits of archival material as documentation of its creator, its time, its place, and the activities it records. Second, they analyze the extent, concentration, and quality of the information, as well as the format in which it is presented, in relation to the quantity of the records. Finally, they judge the adequacy of the repository's resources, especially of staff and space, for arranging, describing, housing, and referencing the archives under consideration.

The methodology of appraisal lies between two irreconcilable facts. On one hand, considered from the perspective of content, almost every document contains a modicum of information that might be useful to some researcher in some circumstance. Moreover, each researcher generally wishes—and legitimately so—to have all material possible on a topic. Because researchers use archives to study topics far beyond the history of the creator, what is glut for one topic may be scarcity for another. Only researchers working on broader, twentieth-century topics find pertinent records in such quantity as to hinder comprehensive research. On the other hand, the merciless, unyielding restriction imposed by the resources of each repository dictate that the archival agencies of the twentieth century cannot retain every record or file. Choices must be made.

The first decision is whether the body of records has a place in the repository. The archivist asks whether the activities, time, and place documented, the adequacy of the documentation, and the richness of content merit inclusion, and whether compatibility with other holdings warrants saving the material. The effective appraiser is knowledgeable enough about the discipline, field, or organization the repository documents to determine whether the group in question contains information previously unavailable or substantially duplicated elsewhere. As archival records provide unique documentation, both of their creator and of events and activities in which the creator was a participant, the good appraiser considers how records under consideration, alone and in conjunction with other groups of records, provide this documentation.

For the second decision, the archivist looks at how well the records document the creator. Some records are richer than others in what Schellenberg termed *evidential* information, data on the origin and organization, policy and procedures, and functions and activities of the creator. Because of the importance of being able to trace the work of a creator and the perspective which that work throws on all the records in the group, archivists routinely retain at least basic evidential documentation.

Certain records may hold little or no data about the creator, but are prized for the data they contain on other persons, places, or events. Case files, which document the population represented in the cases far more than the work of the creator, are a prime example. In assessing this *informational* content, to use Schellenberg's term, the archivist studies the extent and concentration of the information documenting the population.

In the third decision, the archivist reviews various attributes in each body of records being considered. Extensiveness and concentration of information are a function of the form in which financial and statistical data is recorded and of the place of a given record in the documentation of an activity. Certain records largely duplicate the information in other records. Figures entered in daybooks and recorded in receipts at the point of sale are routinely transferred into ledgers and condensed and summarized in annual reports. Before the computer age, researchers unable to do more than accept the analysis of the creator generally preferred records in summary form. Archivists consequently kept the aggregated information and, with space a consideration, normally disposed of bulky receipts. For records created or maintained in machine-readable data bases, however, the opposite is true. Computers give the researcher the power to make all the analyses desired, and summary information that lacks the raw figures from which it was developed is useful only as a record of the creator's analysis of the data. As a result, modern archivists analyze the data base as well as the aggregate presentation.

Records in traditional formats are still in the majority in American archives. Shrewd researchers and archivists know that certain types of material normally contain more information of enduring value than others. Correspondence, minutes, and diaries, for example, usually are more prized by researchers than financial and legal documents because they more fully report the course of events and the part played by their creator than do bank statements, deeds, and the like. Researchers commonly begin analyzing the potential usefulness of a group of records by looking at the quantity and date coverage of the preferred types of material. Archivists assess the value of a body of records in part in terms of the types of material available.

If one appraisal factor is more readily associated with archives than any other, it is age. Yet if archives are defined as records that contain information, rather than as records of a certain vintage, age can never be more than a contributing factor in determining value. In any case, age is a factor defined by use, not by mere chronology. Any chronological demarcation, were it to exist, certainly would have to advance as the years pass. There is no reason to believe that former times are more historically interesting than the present and must be documented more thoroughly, but that in fact may turn out to be the case. The quantity of documentation produced in our time has grown to such staggering proportions that large organizations, following the example of the federal government, report retaining as historically valuable only 2 to 3 percent of all the records generated by or passing through the organization's hands. The tremendous increase can be attributed to several causes, including the creation of such records as the annual income tax for persons who once went undocumented. Records are produced through case files such as those of social service agencies which not only document the formerly undocumented, but create the irony of records that have greater research value in aggregate for statistical analysis of populations than for traditional study of individual cases.

Where records organized in a case-file system clearly have value, but retention of the complete group is beyond the resources of the repository, archivists increasingly are turning to the techniques of sampling. Some believe random sampling of every "nth" file is sufficient because it preserves the characteristics of the files. Others argue that random sampling should be supplemented by selection of files of acknowledged historical interest. Still others suggest that sampling should be done in ways that maintain intact some discrete parts of the record group, e.g., the entire records of a year. Whichever of these methods is chosen, the result preserves the characteristics of the group but sacrifices those records of historical value that do not happen to fall within the sample.

A better method of sampling appears to be that suggested by a major study of the case records of the supreme court of Massachusetts.[2] The study confirmed what many had suspected, that the files which should be preserved are those that contain substantial quantities of records. The "fat file theory" directs that bulkier files, those containing greater quantities of documents, be selected for retention rather than a sampling that includes files holding no more than a few routine forms. "Fat file sampling" preserves the characteristics of the file adequately, while retaining all of those files that have research value for their informational, as well as evidential, content. Researchers working in case files or large bodies of records containing quantities of homogenous files (such as constituent correspondence of legislators and congressmen) should ascertain what, if any, sampling method has been used.

Because of their repetitive nature, records appropriate for sampling are important largely, if not exclusively, for the data they contain. Their value in their original form as objects—archivists use the term *intrinsic value*—is minimal. The vast majority of records in archival repositories possess intrinsic value because their physical form is part of the information they present. Some possess additional intrinsic value because they are fundamental documents (such as the Constitution of the United States or the charter of a corporation) or have questionable characteristics that cannot be studied without reference to the original item. Questionable characteristics, particularly the accuracy of information, require that the researcher must be always alert.

The archivist's job is twofold: first, to document the provenance, or chain of ownership through which the records have passed on their way from creator to archives; and second, to maintain each group of records in a form adequate for study of the authenticity of the items within it. Documenting the history of records is not equivalent to affirming the accuracy of the information within them. Archivists have no way of verifying, nor would they want to vouch for, the accuracy and authenticity of the data in the records. On the contrary, a creator's use of inaccurate or false information in making decisions and conducting affairs is vital information to the researcher, who must reconcile the accuracy of data in the files and the activities of the creator resulting from any inaccurate information.

The job of appraisal, after focusing initially on the records as a group, continues in arranging and describing each newly received group after it has been accessioned. Arrangement, like appraisal, involves a system of choices founded upon the basic principle that each document has, and belongs in, one particular place. The archivist's task is to determine that place within the range of possibilities presented by the system, and to put the document in it. Archivists, unlike managers of *active* files, (the usual term for records during their "first life,") avoid making duplicate copies of documents as cross-references to speed retrieval of the documents and their information. With an unending flow of new accessions, an archival repository finds space even more precious than speed. This means that the researcher must study the finding aids of the repository and consult with the staff in order to make full use of the resources.

Arranging the documents in a group of records consists of two separate but often simultaneous activities: establishing subordinate units within the group and arranging them in an orderly manner. The subordinate units are established in a hierarchical fashion that reflects the relation of each unit to every other unit within the group. To accomplish this, archivists study the contents of the record group to ascertain which units survive as the creator formed them. Those found are normally preserved. Where no such units are evident, archivists create them on the basis of the functions into which the creator's life was divided (career, political involvement, family) or the activities in which the creator participated (chairing a committee or organizing an event). Such groupings usually are discerned easily in the records of organizations, where it is a simple matter to distinguish the records of the president from those of the legal counsel and the comptroller. If neither functions nor activities emerge clearly, archivists then consider forming the subordinate groups on the basis of the ten types of material mentioned previously. Since certain types of material, such as correspondence, often contain richer and more concentrated information of continuing value than others, archivists know that grouping records by type of material directs the researcher to the places in the group in which substantial useful information is likely to be found. Rarely do archivists try to organize records by subject. Few documents, especially correspondence and minutes, discuss only one subject. When there are two or more subjects, the choice of the one of greatest importance by which to identify the document is a judgment which will vary according to the perspective of each reader. Division by chronological period is even less frequently chosen than subject as a basis for grouping records because period indicates neither the work of the creator nor the richness of the documentation present.

The hierarchical level on which principal units within a group are established is called the "series." The series level is the plane on which the creator's original groupings illustrates how the creator categorized and maintained access to the information in the records and reveals the creator's characteristics, interests, and thought. Where "original order" (the original grouping on the series level and subsequent arrangement within the series) is lost, the archivist prefers to organize series by functions or activities of the creator. Doing so reflects the creator's life and work more effectively than other groupings and minimizes the chance of imposing upon the records the interests or perspective of someone other than the creator.

After the material for each unit has been established, it is arranged in an appropriate order. The dictum of the Prussians is followed: where the order established by the creator exists, it is maintained. Where it has been lost, as is often the case with personal papers, archivists create an order employing a combination of three systems: chronology, alphabet, and importance. This is done on each hierarchical level (file unit, series, and intermediate or subseries levels) with awareness of both the material being grouped and the grouping possibilities being considered for the other levels. The intent is to utilize as many of the three categories for grouping as may be useful to define each unit with sufficient exactness to provide the maximum number of access points to the contents of the group.

Since the documents and the folders housing them can be ordered only alphabetically or chronologically, the series level commands the researcher's attention. The order in which the series appears most clearly reveals the organizational pattern in the records. Archivists order the series to exhibit effectively both the nature and content of the group and the work of the creator. This requires ranking the series by the importance, clarity, and fullness of the information in revealing the content in the group as a whole. Specifically, archivists assess: (1) the quantity of documentation present; (2) the chronology represented (the age of the documentation by date of production, not by date of event described); and (3) the closeness of the information to the creator (how personal it is). Since no one characteristic dominates the choice, the first series in order may contain the most personal data, while the second might be the largest in quantity, with neither series necessarily holding the oldest material.

Chronological order is found most consistently on the document and file unit (folder) level, and it is begun anew within each series, if not each subordinate unit within each series. Several decades ago curators of historical manuscript collections thought that organizing all items in chronological order was effective because people's lives are experienced in chronological order. This made it easy to arrange documents by date of creation, and chronological order offered an organization more appropriate than most for individual, unassociated historical manuscripts. However, researchers found chronological organization difficult to use, lacking any grouping whatsoever. Unless a researcher knows the date of an event, a purely chronological arrangement thwarts location of associated documentation because people do not live by chronology alone; they live also by function and activity, each of which proceeds by its own time clock. No longer are entire archives organized exclusively in chronological order. Calendars, which were common only a couple of decades ago, before the proliferation of the photocopy machine, are no longer produced by repositories. They were published to provide access to heavily used material, and ordered each document of a series or record group by date of writing, with a summary of the content. The strict chronological arrangement inhibited the very access that publication promoted.

From record group to record group, the chronological order of items may alternate from straight (earliest to latest) to reverse (latest to earliest). Normally, reverse chronology preserves a modern creator's original order. Active "first life" files often are arranged this way so that the creator can see the latest information first and need study the file only as far back as necessary to refresh memory. Where no order exists and the option of organization is open, the archivist caters to the historical researcher who generally prefers to begin at the beginning.

To describe the arrangement into which a group is ordered, archival repositories produce an *inventory*. This document, the basic form of which was developed by the National Archives of the United States during the decade following its establishment in the mid-1930s, consists of—at best—a minimum of three parts. The first is a physical listing of the units (primarily series and subseries) of the group of records as they are found on the shelf. The physical description typically shows the order, quantity, date, and types of material in each of the component units of the group of records described.

The second part of an inventory is a *scope and content note*. This is the archivist's narrative description of the informational content and the characteristics and special features of the group. The scope and content note focuses on information that is not discernible from study of the physical listing. The note identifies the relationship of the different units to each other in terms of quantity, date, types of material, content, and the like. It provides information that the researcher might be able to glean from prolonged study of the physical listing, but which is too vital for such haphazard acquaintance. Often archivists include, for indexing purposes, a brief list of persons, organizations, events, and other topics prominent in the group of records (whether or not they are prominent in history) not otherwise mentioned in the scope and content note.

The third element of the standard inventory is the creator sketch, a brief history of the organization or biography of the person responsible for the group. This gives the researcher a basis for judging how the documentation reflects the life and activity of the creator. The sketch is not a scholarly treatment, and is intended to provide no more than a perspective.

The archival philosophy of arrangement and description usually gives the researcher two distinct and important means of access to a single group of records. One approach is by the organization of the records. Where units of the group reflect the organizational pattern of the creator, a researcher can, through knowledge of the pattern, locate material of interest. Extending the concept of searching by pattern, the skillful researcher can locate information by exploiting the matrix of hierarchical grouping on the series, file unit, and intermediate levels in combination with the descriptive grouping by function, activity, type of material, and chronology.

The second means of access is through direct indexing. Indexes are of three kinds: those that lead the researcher to a group of records; those that lead to specific documents or items of information with a group; and those that lead to documents housed together because of physical characteristics, such as photographs and maps. The first kind includes chronological and geographical indexes that indicate groups by time periods or regions identified by the repository. The most common index to information is the subject index. Originally created primarily for reference to individual documents within groups of records, subject indexes increasingly are drawn from the data presented in the inventory. When the indexes of several inventories are combined into a union index, a researcher learns of the existence of specific items of information but is deprived of the context within which a desired item rests. The skillful researcher follows the index to a particular inventory to gain that perspective before proceeding to the item.

At present, archival repositories are doing less indexing of holdings than formerly. Overwhelmed by the increasingly large bodies of material generated in the twentieth century, the crowded repositories are forced to devote the lion's share of their descriptive effort to the inventory, the first part of the two-stage descriptive process.

The first contact many researchers have with an archival repository often results from referring to one or both of two important publications that inform users of archival holdings. The first is a guide—often book-length—issued by a repository to give brief, individual descriptions of *all* the record groups it holds. A guide is a listing of contents, record group by record group. Guides are found in many research libraries and especially in archival repositories whose holdings relate to the material described in the guide. Because guides are almost always indexed, they commonly provide the first level of indexing for the user of a repository.

The other publication is the *National Union Catalog of Manuscript Collections (NUCMC)*, produced by the Library of Congress to inform the research community of archival holdings.[3] *NUCMC* entries describe individual groups of records. The entries, which are briefer than those in the guides cited in the preceding paragraph, are grouped first by repository and then ordered alphabetically. The index in the *NUCMC* is essential for locating pertinent record groups in more than one repository. Because automation of the *NUCMC* was not begun until the 1980s, the work presently includes only a fraction of all pertinent groups and it is often overlooked as a starting point in research. Many repositories that have yet to publish a guide contribute information about their holdings to the *NUCMC*, but unfortunately many repositories that should contribute do not. The researcher should remember that failure to find a pertinent group of records listed in the *NUCMC* by no means indicates that such a group does not exist.

A researcher's use of an archives completes the cycle of work put into the records. The work starts with the creator whose activity directly and naturally produces archival material. Next, the archivist works to maintain the integrity and characteristics of the records so that they reflect the creator as faithfully as possible. Finally, the researcher works to discover the meaning of the information in the records from the context of the group in which it is found. By studying the information in a new perspective gleaned from other archival groups, the researcher is able to understand the course and meaning of events more fully than did the creator. History does not just happen. Neither do archives.

FLOYD M. SHUMWAY

3. THE ETHICS
OF ARCHIVAL RESEARCH

Because research libraries are generally the best source of information for beginning users of archival material, most researchers are
destined to spend time in their reading rooms. Both archives and
research libraries can be wonderfully helpful institutions if one
knows how to use them. When starting an extensive project, it is a
good idea to telephone or write in advance of the first visit to
explain what will be needed, and it is common sense and good
practice to establish good working relations with the staff upon
arrival.

The ability to work successfully in any research collection involves, of course, much more than a smile and a handshake on
coming through the door. The researcher must understand that
archives and research libraries have rules, designed not to oppress
users, but to maintain security, create a comfortable atmosphere
for research, preserve the collections, and maintain necessary confidentiality. Users of libraries and archives often resent these rules,
but a researcher cannot function effectively without learning and
following them. Just as houseguests are expected to be courteous
to their hosts, and visitors to an art gallery are watched by guards
who make sure that consideration is shown to the building and the
art objects, the researcher is under an obligation to respect the
established codes of behavior in libraries and archives, recognizing
that they are designed to protect the collections and make them
available to all qualified seekers of information.

Most reseacher collections have printed rules which they present
to newly arrived researchers. Probably no two repositories have
exactly the same requirements, but there is a great deal of similar-
ity, and the regulations described below are typical of those encountered most frequently. Some are simple and based on self-

evident logic. Others are more complex because they involve ethical considerations which may have to be thought through before they can be understood.

Regulations intended to maintain security are certainly understandable. A researcher making an initial trip to a repository must provide acceptable proof of identity and complete a registration form which asks for name, address, nature of the research project, and any affiliation with a college, historical society, or other professional organization. On succeeding visits the researcher simply signs in upon entering the building or reading room. Users of the collection are directed to place coats, briefcases, purses, and other personal property not essential to their work in designated areas, usually a coat room or lockers, to prevent material from the collections being smuggled out of the building in a garment or bag. For the same reason, material being carried by researchers may be inspected by staff when they leave. All archival materials, and the more important or fragile books and periodicals, are kept in closed stacks and the researcher will access those usually by handing in a call slip to a staff person.

Other regulations are designed to assure good working conditions. Only researchers using the collections may work in the reading room; children and spouses of researchers are specifically excluded. Research facilities are not for general study, recreational reading, or loitering. Quiet must be maintained at all times, and smoking is prohibited. The limited, often inadequate, research space is turned over completely to the people who need it so that they can pursue their search for information without distractions.

It is essential that unique and valuable material be protected from damage insofar as is possible, and research collections personnel have found it necessary to place limitations on the manner in which their users conduct their research. Some libraries allow the use of pens, but the great majority permit only pencils, and some even prohibit indelible pencils. Because pencil sharpeners are always found near the users' tables, this is not a troublesome restriction. No beverages or food are allowed in the reading room because they could cause permanent stains on manuscripts and books. To minimize the possibility of damage, researchers are normally given only one box or folder of material at a time, and nothing may be removed from the room.

There are safe ways of handling manuscripts and other archival material. Pages are to be turned carefully, and open volumes should never be placed face down. Researchers are warned against writing in or on books and manuscripts; marking, folding, or otherwise altering records; and placing books, papers, or other objects on research material. Only one folder at a time should be removed from a document case, and individual items should not be taken out of folders. The order of manuscript papers must be preserved. Records which appear to be in disorder must not be rearranged by the researcher but referred to the staff member on duty. Access to records that are of exceptional value or are in fragile condition is always at the discretion of the repository staff, and sometimes typed or microfilmed copies may be substituted for the originals. Manuscripts are used only under direct staff supervision. Book materials are not to be reshelved by the researcher. A volume inadvertently returned to the wrong place is a lost book, and it may remain missing for years, frustrating the staff and disappointing future researchers who wish to use it.

Precautions are also taken to ensure that the public's right to obtain copies of documents or pages of books does not interfere with the institution's need to protect collections from avoidable deterioration. Some repositories have copying facilities available for the reader to use, but the majority require researchers to obtain all photocopies, microfilm, and photographic reproductions from the reference staff. Photocopying of delicate items may be prohibited entirely. Occasionally the researcher will be asked to certify that the requested photocopies are only for private study, research, criticism, or review. It should be noted that photocopying certain materials may be prohibited because of donor restrictions, copyright law, or other legitimate reasons. In most collections, cameras can be brought in and used by researchers only with special permission. This restriction protects materials from damage caused by flashbulbs and keeps other researchers from being distracted by the photographer's movements.

The regulations described up to this point are all based on easily understandable needs that are not subject to different interpretations by different researchers. Users of research material recognize that archives and research libraries strive to protect their collections from theft and misuse and to maintain an atmosphere in which users can work without disturbance. The rules that govern what materials researchers may have access to and what they may publish are more complex because they are based on ethical considerations or restrictions imposed by donors.

Ethics is defined as the discipline dealing with what is good and bad or right and wrong. Although most people want to be good and do the right thing, they frequently have trouble understanding regulations which seem capricious or illogical or both. An established practice may have a benign purpose, but any one who does not understand it may find it merely fussy. A repository may occasionally deny a researcher the right to examine certain documents, and the researcher understandably feels disappointment, if not annoyance. In such instances, usually the researcher is not dealing with rules created by the repository, but rather with rules imposed on the repository by the donor of the material. Researchers feel that they ought to have the right to information, but sometimes donors insist that for one reason or another they must have the right to privacy. Donors can dictate limitations on access to archival material, and the restrictions they establish must be obeyed. Any attempt to circumvent the restrictions becomes an unethical act.

Although archives and research libraries prefer not to have collections partially or totally unavailable to researchers, and though they try to negotiate with donors to permit maximum access for users, they are not always successful. Frequently, donors have valid reasons to worry about misuse of the information in their gift materials. For example, the author of a book or journal article based on the records of a psychiatric clinic could bring terrible and purposeless embarrassment to former patients whose cases were described. Manuscripts or collections of correspondence may contain information which, if published, would damage reputations without adding to public knowledge in any useful way. However, even in such sensitive situations, repositories try to set a limit on the length of time that the information may be kept from qualified investigators.

Permission to examine a manuscript does not constitute permission to publish it in whole or in part. A researcher who wants to use a substantial amount of someone else's work must take proper steps to obtain approval. Failure to identify the source would make the researcher guilty of plagiarism, while identification of the source but failure to get permission would be a breach of ethics. To the extent that they may properly do so, repositories ordinarily grant publication rights to qualified applicants. A written request to publish must be made to the institution which holds the desired material. If permission is granted, the publication must indicate the location of the manuscript, and the author may be required to present a free copy to the owning institution. In giving permission to publish a manuscript, an archives or research library does not surrender its own right thereafter to publish the material itself or to grant permission to others to do so.

In addition to obtaining permission from the repository, sometimes permission must be obtained from the owner of the copyright, who may be the author of the manuscript, or his or her transferee, heirs, legatees, or literary executors. The researcher is expected to be familiar with, or at least aware of, obligations imposed by the laws of libel as well as those protecting literary property rights. Securing the right to publish all or parts of another's manuscript involves legal as well as ethical considerations. Authors may give total access to their manuscripts but limit the way in which the information contained in them can be used. For example, someone presenting a manuscript to a repository may allow the repository to make it freely available for inspection and copying for scholarly purposes, but forbid copying or publishing for financial gain without the author's written approval.

Undertaking research requires attention to regulations, and printed sets of rules are almost always given to new researchers in a repository to indicate appropriate behavior in various possible situations. When using private collections owned by individuals, researchers often must determine appropriate rules of conduct. Private collectors generally have no established policies about use of their materials, but they expect to be treated fairly by researchers whom they invite into their homes to examine special material that they treasure. There can be complex ethical problems, and the researcher is often obliged to invent rules of conduct and then strive to obey them.

To illustrate, the present owner of an inherited eighteenth-century diary might go to considerable trouble to produce a typescript version and generously give copies to a number of people without specifying any limitation on use. Any recipient of the typescript could publish for gain part or all of the text without consulting the owner. An unscrupulous researcher might talk a naive private collector into lending manuscripts and then have them duplicated, even though they were too fragile to be subjected to that treatment. Many other abuses could occur in a relationship between a private collector and someone he has allowed into his home to study his materials. The only real safeguard against such improprieties is the ethical conduct of researchers. A responsible researcher who has been granted access to a private collection will bend over backward to avoid any semblance of misconduct.

JUDITH ANN SCHIFF

4. General Use
of an Archives

Effective use of the resources of an archives depends on good communication between the user and the staff. Successful cooperation between the two will bring forth a productive research strategy. To develop a good collaborative relationship it is essential that the researcher trust the professionalism of the archivist and describe the research project as specifically as possible. Because of the size and complexity of archival collections and the specialized nature of the information sources, a researcher must use catalogs, indexes, and other finding aids with the assistance of an archivist.

Archival research may be compared to mining for precious stones. However, it is a very special kind of prospecting, because all of the stones do not have equal value. The value of each is variable, dependent upon the needs of the researcher and the way in which material is to be utilized. Archivists are indispensable personal guides in the search process. They know the territory, but they can only be effective when they know exactly what the researcher is seeking. The researcher who requests general information on women is at a disadvantage compared to the researcher who requests papers by or about Northern women who taught in the South during and after the Civil War.

If possible, the researcher should write or phone the archives center well in advance of the planned visit. This allows the archivist to provide direct information about the availability of relevant documentation, to recommend other archival repositories, and to prepare for maximum utilization of the center's holdings by the researcher. In some cases, the research may be accomplished without a personal visit, through an oral or written reply or by ordering photocopies of documents. Some archives may provide names of qualified free-lance researchers who may be hired to undertake searching in a particular area of interest.

Even for the researcher who has definitely decided to visit the archives and has obtained information about the center's holdings, it is always advisable to contact the archivist prior to a visit in order to verify service hours, which may be limited or have changed from those published; to allow for sufficient time to retrieve desired materials which may be stored off-site and need to be transported to the reading room; and to ensure that the desired materials are indeed available.

The rules of the archives should be understood by the researcher. Although, following archival standards of practice, repositories should make research materials available on terms of equal access, rules of procedure vary. Almost all archival repositories provide printed rules governing the use of materials.

Upon arrival at the archives, the researcher should be prepared to present full personal identification credentials as required. Most repositories ask for two identification documents, such as a driver's license and an institutional identification card, usually with a photograph attached. For nondrivers, a passport is acceptable identification. A researcher without a photo ID may be required to be photographed on site. Some repositories require a letter of introduction, or a letter of authorization from the donor (or other named agent) of a collection. A few libraries still have educational requirements, such as a bachelor's or doctor's degree for admission. While public institutions generally have few requirements for admission, the researcher at a private institution must be prepared to comply fully with the range of requirements that may be imposed. For example, the researcher may be required to become a member of the institution or to pay a nominal daily-use fee, a practice increasingly common in historical and private societies. Additionally, the researcher may be required to return any photocopies purchased or to submit any writings for approval prior to publication. Researchers should bear in mind that even though regulations may appear discriminatory, they have been adopted by archival repositories to ensure that resources remain intact and available for continued use by future researchers. In any case, the staff is carrying out the established policy of the institution, and it is not beneficial to the research process to try to evade or protest any requirements at the time of the visit.

In addition to personal registration, the researcher is routinely required to complete an application to examine archival material. It is usually stated that by signing the application form, the researcher agrees to abide by the rules regulating use of the material. The application usually requests a description of the subject and purpose of the research project. Examples of projects are: to examine town vital records for use in preparing a family tree; to examine the records of nineteenth-century women's clubs to write a senior term paper; and to examine the papers of a senator in order to write a full biography. The archivist reviews the application and interviews the researcher about the proposed project in order to provide the greatest amount of information from the available documentation. The researcher should be prepared to explain the research subject both specifically and generally and to describe the primary and secondary sources already examined. If the research topic is the Second Seminole War, it should be named specifically, and then placed in historical perspective, citing date span, geographical sites, and principal organizations and individuals involved. The archivist may not find any material listed as relating to the Second Seminole War, but by checking the names of participants may find that a full narrative account is included in the collected papers of a New England family.

Beyond providing ready reference help with source materials, the archivist will explain the use of the center's finding aids to the researcher. The range of finding aids extends from handwritten calendars received with collections to on-line national data bases linking the holdings of many repositories. Pertinent catalogs, indexes, special subject guides, and finding aids for individual collections or groups will be explained. The standard guide to individual collections is the register or inventory which is described in chapter 2.

In addition to rules on the use of archival materials, most repositories have rules for the use of the reading room. The unique nature of archival materials confers both privileges and responsibilities on the user. The physical nature of the material requires careful handling to maintain its integrity and minimize deterioration. Researchers should expect to be subject to the following standard rules, especially in larger archives:

1. Coats, hats, brief cases, typewriter cases, books, and all other personal property except notecards and pencils must be checked while the researcher is using archival material. Purses will be inspected upon leaving. No materials may be left overnight in the reading room or checkroom.
2. The use of pens or indelible pencils is not permitted. Typewriters, personal tape recorders, and computers are usually permitted.
3. Notecards no larger than 5" × 8" may be used in the reading room. Larger sized paper and pads are not permitted. Specially marked paper is provided for researchers without charge.
4. No materials may be removed from the reading room.
5. Materials must be handled with care. No markings may be added or erased, and no tracing or rubbings may be made. No objects may be placed on archival materials. Materials should be kept in their original order within the folders; filing errors should be reported to a staff member.
6. Researchers may not make photocopies of archival materials. Photocopies and photographs may be ordered in accordance with designated rules.
7. All materials must be returned to the service desk. The researcher should notify a staff member when use of the material has been finished.
8. Smoking and eating are not permitted in the reading room.

Researchers sometimes ask why valuable archival materials are not published or photocopied for permanent preservation. Many repositories do microfilm portions of their holdings as resources permit, but even the thousands of reels of microfilm prepared by the National Archives represent only a portion of its holdings. Especially valuable or fragile items are usually given priority for photocopying. Although papers of selected public figures and organizations are published, most archival materials will never be photoduplicated; there are too many documents of limited and specialized use, and new records are constantly being generated. Various conservation and preservation methods have been used to protect archival materials, ranging from old techniques such as the silking of manuscripts to the new techniques of mylar encapsulation. (See chapter 14.)

During the research interview the archivist may ask if the researcher wishes to communicate with other researchers working on a similar topic. Some repositories have a form for this purpose, while others share information informally. A researcher who wishes to be put in contact with other researchers should request this and leave with the archivist a written statement describing the research project. Most archivists will not discuss one researcher's project with another researcher without permission, because of the risk of violating confidentiality.

If a research visit lasts more than one day, the researcher should maintain frequent contact with the archivist because additional sources and points of access which are not in the finding aids may come to the archivist's mind. It is recommended that researchers inquire if there are other staff members with expertise in the area of investigation. Archivists who are subject specialists can be of invaluable assistance.

An exit interview with the archivist can be as important to the researcher as the initial meeting. Many researchers who are pressed for time work in the reading room until the center closes, but it is often more important to save time for a final meeting with the archivist before departing permanently. An exit interview benefits not only the researcher and future researchers but the archives center as well. During the interview the researcher reviews the project, discusses the relevant source materials utilized, points out special strengths and weaknesses in the collections, and requests any necessary follow-up.

The exit interview is the time to discuss questions relating to publication of the research project—such as copyright, credit lines, and publication fees—and to obtain any special forms to be submitted to the archives in the future. If the researchers's visit was not long enough to allow examination of all relevant material, the researcher should advise the archivist of any plans to revisit the repository.

If time does not permit an exit interview, or if the archivist is not available, the researcher should contact the archivist later by telephone or letter. A thank-you letter citing staff members who were especially helpful will be greatly appreciated and may facilitate future research contacts with the archives center.

As more unpublished materials become accessible through automated processing techniques, microform publications, and data bases, finding all the sources relevant to a research project becomes increasingly complex. Rather than allowing the researcher to reduce reliance on the staff of the archives center, this proliferation of source materials has made efficient, thorough searches dependent more than ever upon expert guidance.

Private Manuscript Sources

Although the terms *manuscripts* and *archives* are used interchangeably to describe documentary records having historical or literary significance, *manuscripts* generally refers to private papers, and *archives* to official or organizational records. Private manuscript sources may include groups of personal papers with an organic unity (those of an individual or family), artificial collector's collections devoted to a special subject (the Civil War or Charles Lindbergh), and individual documents of special importance (the diary of a colonial blacksmith or farmer).

Legally, private papers belong to an individual and are disposed of in accordance with the individual's wishes. In actuality, an individual's private papers may include a series of official records, such as the records of an organization in which the individual served as an officer. Conversely, organizational records may include private papers, such as those of a professor which were left in a departmental office and became incorporated into the college archives. Sometimes the right to own or dispose of an individual's records becomes the subject of legal controversy, as exemplified by the papers of President Richard Nixon and those of Emily Dickinson.

The types of personal papers accumulated by an individual over a lifetime are as varied as individual lifestyles. What survives for future acquisition by a repository is subject to fire, flood, decay, and other disasters. Older collections may include legal papers, such as deeds and indentures, household inventories, diaries, receipts, and letterbooks. Modern collections may include photographs, tape recordings, videotapes, and machine-readable records. Even printed material (travel literature, theater programs, newspaper clippings) may be incorporated into a collection of personal papers. The private papers of an individual may also include school notebooks, report cards and diplomas, financial records such as bills, cancelled checks and tax returns, deeds, wills, professional papers brought home from the office, and such personal papers as diaries, medical records, and love letters.

Examples of the many possible varieties of private papers which may be found in a collection are included in the papers of the noted twentieth-century geographer, Ellsworth Huntington. A substantial portion of his papers are comprised of materials relating to his geographical expeditions, which took him to the American southwest and northwest, the Middle East, and China. There are letters to local scholars and officials detailing the arrangements for his field trips, maps and informational materials, photographs and negative files, logs of his photographs, field notebooks, and research materials collected at the sites. Huntington was also a university professor for many years, and his papers include teaching materials, lecture notes, grade books, and correspondence with his colleagues and university administrators. Huntington was a prolific and popular author of books and articles, and much in demand as a public lecturer. In addition to drafts and copies of his completed works, there are incomplete drafts, and research files pertaining to a variety of topics. The research files include notes and printed material which he collected, as well as material sent to him by others.

In addition to his primary work in geography, Huntington was a leading figure in the eugenics movement of the 1920s and 1930s. The subject files of his papers include records kept as a director of the American Eugenics Society and an extensive correspondence file, amounting to over 5000 pieces, from the 1930s which includes letters exchanged with Margaret Sanger and Paul Popenoe. Huntington served in both world wars in intelligence and research capacities, and his records reveal military concerns involving the environment, weather, and clothing. He also worked for the development of the United Nations, contributing to the writing of its charter and lobbying for its adoption. Most of the 318 archival boxes of his papers, however, are filled with correspondence with the major geographers and historians of the twentieth century, including Arnold Toynbee, James Harvey Robinson, James Bryce, and Frederick Jackson Turner. The number of persons and subjects which are documented in this collection of private papers extends into the thousands, and as new historical specializations evolve, the papers will provide "new" sources for scholarly investigation.

Private papers provide endless fascination and also problems for the archivist and the researcher. While they have organic unity reflecting the life experiences and interests of an individual, they usually have not been kept systematically. A single document may describe a number of subjects, and interest in—or even recognition of—a subject changes with time. It has been said that history has to be rewritten in every generation. A corollary might be that historical sources should be reviewed and redescribed in every generation. For example, the papers of a colonial aristocrat containing carefully cataloged letters of famous early Americans may have new interest because of the previously passed over uncataloged records of his apprentices, domestic servants, or slaves.

An author's papers are important because they contain early drafts of writings, research, and idea files revealing the growth of the author's literary thought. Of special interest are unpublished revisions and drafts which may provide material for new editions and reevaluations of the author's contributions to literary culture.

Private papers kept by assistants to notable persons often provide supplementary documentation and unique firsthand perceptions. This type of personal collection is usually small in size and may be overlooked by researchers, especially when the papers of a prominent individual are voluminous. The extra investment of time taken to check for any papers which may have been saved by an aide can often yield profits in the form of a better understanding of the notable personality and his or her working habits and lifestyle. This material may well result in an improved end product article or essay for the researcher. William Howard Taft, for example, left an enormous collection of official and personal papers which the Library of Congress has microfilmed. The microfilm publication of several hundred reels is held by a number of libraries, but it is too large to be read in its entirety. Even the process of selecting relevant reels for examination may be staggering.

Be that as it may, Taft's private secretary, Wendell L. Mischler, kept a small collection of his own papers, mainly in the form of letters exchanged with his wife and some correspondence with Taft. These letters constitute an almost daily record of the activities of both men, especially for the period 1913–1921, after Taft's presidency and prior to his appointment to the United States Supreme Court. Mischler's letters provide documentation of Taft's busy schedule as a professor and public lecturer, and explain how he was able to accomplish so much through the efficient organization of his work. Beyond that, the correspondence contains information on the history of business technology, as it was during this period that Mischler first tested and enthusiastically recommended the purchase of the latest invention, a dictating machine.

During this same period of American political history, while the Democratic Party occupied the White House, Frances B. Denton was responsible for keeping the diary of Colonel Edward M. House, President Wilson's advisor and confidant. Colonel House was the controversial head of the American delegation to the Paris Peace Conference at the end of World War I. "Miss Fannie," a close friend of the House family, and the colonel's personal secretary, arranged his daily schedule and accompanied him on every one of his extended trips. House publicly acknowledged his debt to her, for without her he would not have dictated the diary, which has become one of the keystone primary historical records of the twentieth century. Unfortunately for the historian, Denton was so conscious of her sensitive and confidential role, that she maintained no sizable personal collection of her own papers. Some of her letters, shorthand notebooks, and memorabilia, including some photographs of Colonal House, were, however, preserved by her favorite niece, who thoughtfully donated them to the House archive years after Miss Fannie's death.

The papers of a military aide to the outstanding statesman Henry L. Stimson have recently been donated as an adjunct to the Stimson papers by the children of Eugene A. Regnier. A career army officer, Regnier served as Stimson's aide while he was governor-general of the Philippines in the 1920s, secretary of state under Herbert Hoover, and secretary of war under Franklin D. Roosevelt. These as yet unpublished papers include valuable insights on Regnier's efforts to improve relations between the State Department and the press, on Stimson's administration of the State and War Departments, and other matters. They will add a new dimension of understanding of American foreign policy for the period between the wars.

Diaries and account books, journals, and logs are often kept and saved alone without related correspondence and papers. While there may not be enough research material in any one volume by itself, or even in an individual series, to support a study, together in a collection their significance is enhanced. Archival repositories may specialize in the collecting of particular subject volumes such as Civil War diaries, whaling logs, or farming account books. In groups, the documentation may provide substantial evidence for analyses of change over time in various topics. For example, the numbers and group movements of whales and seals from the early to the mid-nineteenth century may be determined from the examination of a large sample group of whaling logs. Or, the variety of farm operations performed and managed by women may be determined from examining farming account books. Changing practices in child rearing may be described in family diaries. One example of a special subject collection is the collection of diaries, memoirs, and other papers kept by missionaries to China which has been formed at the Yale Divinity School Library. Through outreach and cooperative efforts, the China Records Project has acquired the material of over 300 individuals covering the period 1834–1978.

Diaries and other genre records kept over the years by an individual also provide documentation for comparative studies. The journals of a navy surgeon, kept in voluminous detail by Dr. Benajah Ticknor from 1818 through 1852, contain fascinating commentaries on early American visits to China in the 1830s and 1840s. Also described is Ticknor's first sampling of Chinese food, which he found to be both tasty and nutritious. Ticknor's voyages took him to every continent, where he had opportunities to observe and analyze the movement for independence in South America, American attempts to conclude a commercial treaty with Japan in 1846, and missionary activities in Hawaii. Along the way, he commented on the drunkenness, disease, and disciplinary problems aboard ship.

The beginnings of the United States' ties to Hawaii are strikingly documented in the papers of the Hiram Bingham family, in letters and biographical writings of the early nineteenth-century missionary. They are brought to life most poignantly in the diary of his wife, Sybil Moseley Bingham. Hiram Bingham, a Middlebury College alumnus, felt the call to convert the native population of the Hawaiian Islands. He had fallen under the spell of Yale's evangelical preacher-president, Timothy Dwight, the Younger, and had also taught Indian and Hawaiian youths at the missionary school in Cornwall, Connecticut. Bingham was a bachelor, however, and the missionary board appointed only married men to serve abroad. Less than two weeks prior to the scheduled sailing date of the missionary ship from Boston, in 1819, Bingham met a spinster missionary who also strongly desired to convert and teach the native children. A fortuitous match was made, and Sybil's diary frankly describes her love and dedication to her faith and to her husband. It records also her self-doubts and her experiences of twenty-one years in Hawaii, teaching and converting the Hawaiian Queen Kaahumanu, and bringing other features of American civilization and culture to the islands, including dress, manners, and architecture.

Cherished collections of handwritten recipe books provide ample evidence of the great amounts and variety of food and medical preparations for which the homemakers of the past were responsible. Often the volumes are written in several different hands as they were passed lovingly from one generation to another. Recipes for breads, meats, and sweets predominate, but there are also many recipes for wines, beer, and cordials, as well as for poultices, liniments, and internal medications. Formulas for cleaning preparations for clothing and household were usually included as well. Researchers of today cannot always make direct use of older recipes, however, as not only do the measuring standards differ, but directions for making the basic sauces or processes the well-trained cook was assumed to know were often omitted.

Diaries of "ordinary women" attest to the unrelenting schedules for household work which had to be followed. Even women with domestic help were kept actively busy. Cooks and maids in labor-scarce America had to be recruited, trained, and rigorously supervised, and some diaries provide evidence that the lady of the house often worked along with her hired help in large jobs such as canning and pickling.

One's own letter filebox or trunk can sometimes prove to be a source of archival treasures. Some families have carefully preserved old family letters and records, and consciously passed them down from one generation to another. Often the family is unaware that its own archive may also be of interest and importance to others outside the family. With the transient lifestyle of most modern families, significant accumulations of manuscripts and memorabilia must often be quickly disposed of either by donation or by destruction. When an elderly relative or perhaps a matriarch or patriarch dies, such treasures are too often set out with the trash by unknowing or uncaring descendants, or left behind for the next occupant of an old house to deal with.

The local library or historical society can provide some information on the value of personal papers as source material, and can suggest other institutions and experts for further information. It is essential that the individual who owns the material provide as much information about it as possible so that a consultant or potential repository can appropriately evaluate it. The material should be reviewed as a whole; it is not desirable to divide it into splinter collections by persons or subjects. Consider the collection as a kind of family portrait through time, not just as grandfather's World War I diary or grandmother's school papers and dance programs. Portions which appear to the uninitiated to seem trivial or "purely personal" should not be weeded out or discarded. The elimination of some material can always be done later with the advice of experts, whereas some potentially valuable material might be destroyed. A general inventory should be prepared by boxes or folders, not necessarily down to the item level. Note should be made of the person who kept the papers, the subjects described, special formats such as photographs or clippings, the time span covered by the material, the size of the collection estimated in linear or shelf feet, and the physical condition, e.g., mildewed or brittle condition. Items of special importance or interest should be noted.

The consulting librarian or archivist should be provided with a written copy of the inventory, so that the owner may be advised as fully as possible about repositories which may be interested in the collection or individual items within it. A professional archivist should advise not only on his or her repository's interest in the material, but should also advise of other repositories which may have related collections. A donation *may* have tax deductible value, though of course, many do not. If this is a consideration, further information must be sought from the librarian or archivist, a legal or financial professional, or the Internal Revenue Service. By law, monetary evaluations of donations cannot be prepared by the archives staff, but lists of names of qualified professional appraisers are available. Appraisers must be selected and paid by the donor of the material, not the receiving repository.

One does not have to inherit an old family archives to be the holder of important archival documentation. Special subject collections are often accumulated by an individual through participation in an activity such as a reform movement, an expedition, an investigation, or by having been an eyewitness to an event such as a civil rights demonstration or a natural disaster. A massive Kent State Collection has been compiled through the efforts of several authors and journalists who studied and investigated the killings which took place at the university in May of 1970. They obtained copies of relevant FBI files through the Freedom of Information Act, interviewed witnesses and family members, and solicited documentation collected by others. Letters sent home by a child in summer camp, or by a college student, may provide useful documentation for social historians. Most college and university archives welcome donations of letters, diaries, lecture notebooks, and personal record books kept by their alumni.

Listings of manuscript repositories may be found in directories, catalogs, and databases. Two standard publications which are most helpful in identifying repositories by location and specialization are the *Directory of Archives and Manuscript Repositories in the United States,* published by the National Historical Publications and Records Commission in 1978, and *Subject Collections: A Guide to Special Book Collections and Subject Emphases as Reported by University, College, Public and Special Libraries and Museums in the United States and Canada* compiled by Lee Ash and William G. Miller, with the collaboration of Barbara J. McQuitty, 6th edition, 1985. The repositories are listed in the *Directory* by state and alphabetically by city and town under each state, and indexed by subject holdings. *Subject Collections* is comprised of two volumes of subject listings in one dictionary-style alphabetical listing.

If the material to be offered to a repository deals with a number of subjects, the locale of the family or organization documented is a good place to search for possible repositories. If the family whose affairs are documented in the material lived primarily in Fairfield, Connecticut, for example, it would be advisable to find out if any local societies or libraries are listed in either of these two guidebooks. The *Directory* lists three repositories under this town: the Fairfield Historical Society; the Fairfield Public Library; and Fairfield University. Each listing contains brief descriptions of holdings and of materials solicited. If no local repository is listed, or if the description does not seem to cover the type of material being offered, the listings of repositories in the capital city or larger nearby city should be checked.

When the collected papers relate to one subject, or a few disparate subjects, another approach would be to seek out one or more repositories which specialize in the relevant subject(s). If, for example, the papers of a family member who served in the Spanish-American War have been preserved, comprised perhaps of letters home, orders, and a few photographs, both the *Directory* and *Subject Collections* may be searched. The *Directory* lists ten repositories under the heading, "Spanish-American War," and *Subject Collections* lists four under the heading, "U.S. History—War of 1898." In the latter listings, the University of Connecticut Library is cited with one uncataloged collection of manuscripts of an individual who was active in the Philippines and Spain, while the New York Public Library and the West Point Library describe only book and map collections. The last listing is the United States Army Military History Institute, Carlisle Barracks, Pennsylvania, which holds a cataloged manuscript collection comprised of 2500 folders and fifty boxes titled "The Spanish-American War Survey." It consists of "personal letters, diaries, and recollections of regular and volunteer servicemen in all areas of service" and is described as being "the largest collection in the world of personal papers of American servicemen at the turn of the century." On the other hand, although the *Directory* lists ten repositories, the specialized collection at the Carlisle Barracks is not indexed under "Spanish-American War."

If the collection which the owner wishes to donate is composed of letters and immigration papers of Polish-American ancestors, for example, one finds twenty repositories specializing in collecting

Polish-American materials in *Subject Collections* and six listed in the *Directory*. Both list the primary national institutions: the Polish Museum of America in Chicago, and the Jozef Pilsudski Institute for Research in the Modern History of Poland in New York. Others listed have American regional specializations which should also be taken into account in offering one's collection to a repository.

During the last generation of historical investigation, social history has gained a new stature and definition. Previously used primarily to describe lifestyles and leisure activities, social history now studies and analyzes the organization and change of social classes, groups, and the family over a period of time. History is no longer seen as the product only of the activities of great men and women but as the product of many interactive groups. The "common" individual in the group has recently captured the attention of historical investigators, from professional academic historians to amateur family historians. Social history is a newly recognized field of public history whose researchers include government historians, museum curators, archivists, and historical society staff dedicated to making historical records and material culture accessible to the general public. The celebration of the bicentennial of the United States Constitution is one reflection of the heightened public interest in history and the historical record. Through the examination and analysis of the private sources of history which are available in local repositories in the original or microform copies, researchers can better understand and appreciate our past and its effect on our present and our future. Much of the material is there to be used because people from all walks of life took the trouble to save it, and when the right time came, to donate it to the place in which it would be most useful to the greatest number of people. Librarians, especially those in public and college libraries, but often in special libraries too, can be of inestimable help in steering would-be donors in the right direction.

5. ARCHIVAL REFERENCE TOOLS

The basic reference tools used by the researcher working with archival materials are available in most research and large public libraries, although they will not be found on the shelves of every archives. An archives or manuscript collection can rarely afford to purchase all potentially relevant reference works, particularly if they are readily available in a nearby collection.

Archives concern themselves with historical information. A practicing archivist rarely consults the current volume of *Who's Who*, but often needs volumes from the 1920s and 1930s. Important tools in archival collections concerned with state government include government organizational manuals, directories, and civil lists from the nineteenth century. Researchers needing to know how the government functioned in both 1848 and 1948 will routinely use older copies of standard reference sources considered to be out of date by most libraries.

Researchers using historical documents, whether manuscript or printed, must avoid making anachronistic assumptions about the past. The meanings of words, place names, and popular perceptions change over time. A person attempting to locate places named in a nineteenth century diary may be misled by a modern atlas.

One of the major differences between primary manuscript sources in archives and printed source materials is the localism of the former: letters, diaries, and other manuscripts. An important historical figure writing a pamphlet or memoir is writing to a broad audience. One assumes that allusions and references in a public statement by George Washington or Benjamin Franklin were understood by reasonably educated people of their time. However, private letters, diaries, and records of even the most important historical figures are filled with references to local people and places. A person reading Washington's public statements can be expected to be familiar with the political controversies of Washington's time, but a researcher studying Washington's private papers may have to become familiar with the names of his neighbors, friends, relatives, slaves, and business associates, and with obscure Virginia place names and eighteenth-century agricultural practices. The names of Washington's political or military associates can be found in such standard reference works as the *Dictionary of American Biography* or the *Biographical Directory of the American Congress,* but it is more difficult to establish the identity of his second cousin.

Local Sources

A regional history collection should provide quick access to published local histories. A collection of local histories is almost always in constant use despite the variation in quality of individual works, particularly for biographical information about important local figures. Local histories were often written by amateurs, some of whom were excellent reporters and historians while others were inaccurate, credulous, and biased. A history that gives detailed listings of the names of first settlers and elected officials and clearly recounts the histories of Civil War regiments may neglect to mention late nineteenth-century labor unrest and the activities of new immigrant groups. Because a subject is not mentioned in a local history does not mean it did not exist.

A good starting point for identifying local histories is *United States Local Histories in the Library of Congress: A Bibliography,* edited by Marion J. Kaminkow. There are also state and regional bibliographies of local histories, including reference works that cite articles in periodicals. Local histories are in great demand by historians and genealogists, and are often reprinted, sometimes with added indexes of names.

The most useful local sources may be unpublished indexes to newspapers. A researcher should check libraries and historical societies for subject or obituary indexes to newspapers.

Using and Understanding Manuscripts

The researcher using manuscripts from before the mid-nineteenth century will encounter problems not generally found in printed works, but a number of guides to research provide help. The *Harvard Guide to American History* includes brief but valuable comments on understanding colonial handwriting, dating manuscripts, and editing. Two publications of the Manuscript Society, although aimed primarily at autograph and manuscript collectors, contain useful information, particularly on the identification of manuscripts by important historical figures. *Manuscripts: The First Twenty Years* is a compilation of articles which appeared in the journal *Manuscripts* from 1948 to 1968, with some updating of information; *Autographs and Manuscripts: A Collector's Manual* contains several helpful articles. Genealogical manuals may also include information on using manuscript materials, including legal and governmental records. *The Source: A Guidebook of American Genealogy* is perhaps the most comprehensive guide, with extensive bibliographical references. Among the useful publications of the American Association for State and Local History is H. G. Jones's *Local Government Records: An Introduction to Their Management, Preservation, and Use.*

Researchers using older documents, particularly those dating from the colonial period, may have difficulty in deciphering the handwriting. Often reading historical documents is simply a matter of becoming familiar with a particular person's handwriting, but documents from the seventeenth, eighteenth, and early nineteenth century exhibit handwriting styles different from today's.

Colonial diaries and letters contain some letter forms no longer used. The *long s,* formed like an *f* in both printing and handwriting, is familiar. In reproductions of the Declaration of Independence and of the Constitution, *Congress* appears to be written as *Congreſs.* Some letter forms are easily misread. The eighteenth-century capital *S* can be confused with *L,* so that *Lockport* can be misread as *Stockport.* The most commonly misinterpreted letter is the thorn, written as *y,* which stands for *th.* *Ye tavern* is actually *the* tavern. Official government and legal documents written in "secretary hand" are particularly difficult to interpret. Some handbooks for genealogists, such as Val D. Greenwood's *Researcher's Guide to American Genealogy,* include brief instructions for reading old script. Separate publications on reading early handwriting include E. Kay Kirkham's *How to Read the Handwriting and Records of Early*

America and Harriet Stryker-Rodda's *Understanding Colonial Handwriting.*

The meaning of a word can shift over time. The *Oxford English Dictionary,* although based on British rather than American usage, is helpful in explaining earlier word meanings and includes dated examples. *Webster's Ninth New Collegiate Dictionary* cites the date of the earliest known use of a word in the sense that is used today.

Before the mid-nineteenth century, several systems of spelling were in use in America. A person using *Walker's Dictionary* as an authority wrote *Almanack* while *Webster's dictionary* preferred *Almanac.* Variant spellings in older documents do not necessarily mean that the writer was uneducated. Researchers using older dictionaries should be aware of the common differences in spelling.

Researchers using older materials are likely to encounter forms of measurement which are archaic, or at least not in general use today. Older arithmetic texts and dictionaries can assist with various measures and units of currency.

A perpetual calendar is valuable in establishing dates of letters and other manuscript materials. Often dates are incomplete. As an example, some family papers contain a letter referring to Abraham Lincoln, and it is clear from the context that Lincoln was then the president, but the letter is incompletely dated as Tuesday, April 8. A perpetual calendar reveals that in the 1860s, April 8 fell on Tuesday in 1862, providing the probable date of the letter—assuming that the writer did not err in writing the date. A perpetual calendar is included in Kenneth Duckett's *Modern Archives,* but they can also be found in almanacs, encyclopedias, and research handbooks. Before England and the British colonies adopted the Gregorian calendar in 1753, the year began on March 25. However, because other countries had already adopted the Gregorian calendar, which used January 1 as the beginning of the year, English documents were often dated with a dual year statement, such as February 3, 1690/91. Anyone working with documents written before 1753 should become familiar with the earlier dating system. The *Harvard Guide to American History* and several other research and genealogical handbooks offer clear explanations of British colonial dating practices.

Financial records during the colonial period and, in some cases, as late as the mid-nineteenth century, will refer to the older English form of pounds, shillings, and pence. The colonial period can be quite confusing because of the various currencies in use. After 1790, the United States government, and most merchants, adopted the less confusing decimal currency in use today, but farmers and others persisted in using the old form of currency in their account books. Account books from western New York were kept in the old "York" money in the 1830s and 1840s, and prices were expressed in shillings through the 1860s, more than seventy years after the old state currencies were replaced in law by "federal money." The key to converting York to federal money can be found in early nineteenth-century arithmetic text books, which carried instructions for converting money from one system to the other.

Contemporary arithmetic textbooks are also useful sources for older measuring systems. This author keeps a copy of Roswell Smith's *Practical and Mental Arithmetic* (1843) on hand in case it is necessary to know how many gallons of cider are in a barrel (61½) and how many barrels are in a hogshead (two). Most arithmetic textbooks of the period include similar information.

Geographical Reference Works

References to place names may require some detective work because place names change. The New York counties of Charlotte (named after George the Third's Queen) and Tyron (named after the Royal Governor) were renamed after Revolutionary War heroes Washington and Montgomery in 1784. In the 1960s, many streets were renamed to honor John F. Kennedy and Martin Luther King, Jr. Villages that were once important trade centers have dwindled or disappeared.

Political jurisdictions also change. The state of Maine was once part of Massachusetts. Parts of Vermont were once claimed by both New York and New Hampshire. A resident of Buffalo, New York, between 1804 and 1821 was successively a resident of Ontario, Genesee, Niagara, and Erie counties. While a modern atlas is useful in research, current place names should be checked against contemporary sources. Recently, a researcher was trying to identify the author of a series of letters written in the 1820s that were sent from various locations in Upper Canada, now Ontario. The letters came from Beverly, Blenheim, Oxford, and Burford. A modern road atlas located Blenheim some fifty miles east of Detroit-Windsor. When the other three names were not found, the researcher went to the Canadian history section of the library and found a description of Upper Canada, written in the 1820s, which included a map. Beverly, Blenheim, Oxford, and Burford were all identified as townships between the modern cities of Hamilton and London, Ontario. The Blenheim on the 1820 map was more than one hundred miles from the Blenheim in the 1985 road atlas.

There are several sources for locating maps. Volumes 1–4 and 7–8 of *A List of Geographical Atlases in the Library of Congress,* and the *Dictionary Catalog of the Map Division* of the New York Public Library, both provide information about thousands of national, state, city, and regional atlases. The American Geographical Society *Index to Maps in Books and Periodicals* is a guide to maps not included in the lists from the Library of Congress and New York Public Library. Richard Sealock's *Bibliography of Place-Name Literature in the United States, Canada, Alaska, and Newfoundland* provides information on names, name changes, and lists of gazetteers.

Biographical Information

Personal papers and manuscripts are often filled with the names of family members, business associates, friends, politicians, and others. It is not unusual for a diary to mention two or three hundred people in the course of a year. While many references in diaries or in family letters are passing mentions of neighbors or local merchants, it is often necessary to establish the identity of relatively obscure individuals. Who is the Sally Ann mentioned in the diary of a farmer in the 1840s? Is she wife or child, hired woman or teacher? Diaries also contain references to important figures, such as a lecture by a noted author or the death of a president. The death date of Daniel Webster or Henry Clay may be the key to dating an undated letter or manuscript.

Information on important historical figures appears in the *Dictionary of American Biography, National Cyclopaedia of American Biography, Who's Who,* and other standard reference works. The *Biog-*

raphy and Genealogy Master Index locates biographical information in current and historical biographical sources. Researchers should be careful of assumptions about the identity of names encountered in manuscript collections. It may seem natural to assume that a John Hancock letter was written by the signer of the Declaration of Independence, although several John Hancocks lived in colonial Massachusetts, including one of the most prominent merchants of the time. Collections of autographs are often filled with such mistaken identities. For a person with a John Hancock letter, a biographical source might be the first step in determining whether the letter was written by *the* John Hancock. Some similar "confused identities" are discussed in *Autographs and Manuscripts: A Collector's Manual,* Mary Benjamin's *Autographs: A Key to Collecting,* and several books by Charles Hamilton.

Many reference works of collective biographies exist. There are directories of military figures, governors, mayors, physicians, university faculties, and seemingly almost any identifiable professional or occupational group. Especially popular with researchers are the political directories. It sometimes seems that everyone has either held public office, or is related to someone who held public office. References to political events and personalities occur frequently in personal papers even where there is no direct family or personal connection. The *Biographical Directory of the American Congress, 1774–1971* is a standard source, and there are many directories of state and local political figures. The government manuals of most states list state officeholders and provide biographical information on legislators and other officials; former governors and former legislators may be included, also.

Biographical directories which deal with a precisely defined group, such as the United States Congress, can be expected to be comprehensive. Other works, such as the *Dictionary of American Biography,* depend upon the judgment of their editors to determine who is historically important and worthy of inclusion. Contemporary biographical directories, particularly those listing professionals, usually ask the biographees to supply personal information by means of questionnaires. Nevertheless, many people eligible for inclusion object to having their names appear and refuse requests for biographical information.

Local histories, particularly those published in the last half of the nineteenth century, regularly include useful biographical sketches, even though the information was often supplied by family members, thus reflecting what the family thought important. Sometimes people paid to be represented in a local history. Because of frequent use by local historians and genealogists, the reprint editions of these works occasionally include name indexes, or separately published name indexes may be available.

Most biographical publications, with the exception of local histories, do not include information about the subject's family. Family relationships can be critical for understanding the papers of a historical figure. Sometimes genealogies can provide the needed clues, as in the following example of the genealogy of Eliab W. Capron of Williamstown, New York. In the early 1840s, Capron wrote a series of letters critical of the Quakers to the abolitionist newspaper, the *Liberator,* and publicly resigned his membership in the Society of Friends. In 1850, Capron published one of the first works on spiritualism in Auburn, New York. The researcher found a family genealogy at the Buffalo and Erie County Public Library that identified three men named Eliab W. Capron, two of whom (cousins) lived in central New York. Records kept by the Society of Friends established that the man who resigned from the Society was the son of David and Laban Capron. A manuscript collection at the University of Rochester included letters concerning spiritualism written from Auburn, New York, in 1850, by Eliab W. Capron and Rebecca M.C. Capron. From the context of the letters, the researcher could safely assume that Eliab W. Capron and Rebecca Capron were closely related and that this Eliab was the Capron who wrote the spiritualist tract. Returning to the genealogy, the researcher found that the Capron who was the son of David and Laban (the Quaker) had married a Rebecca Cooper. Capron, the ex-Quaker, could thus be linked with Capron, the spiritualist.

Guides to genealogies are plentiful. Two important ones were edited by Marion J. Kaminkow: *Genealogies in the Library of Congress: A Bibliography,* and a companion volume, *A Complement to Genealogies in the Library of Congress* which describes twenty thousand genealogies in forty-five major libraries not included in the first title.

City directories are valuable for quick identification of individuals. As an example, a researcher was attempting to verify a statement in the obituary of his great-grandfather that he had practiced medicine in Buffalo, New York, from 1848–1853. Rather than turning immediately to local histories or checking older directories of physicians, the researcher consulted city directories for the 1840s and 1850s to establish that the man had practiced medicine in Buffalo. For this search, the information included in the city directory was sufficient. If the researcher wanted to pursue this further, he probably would have been able to find his great-grandfather's name in other sources, because physicians are relatively well documented. Had his grandfather been a bricklayer or laborer, the Buffalo city directory might have been the only printed reference to verify his existence. Most of the city directories listed in Dorothea Spear's *Bibliography of American Directories through 1860* have been microfilmed by Research Publications, Inc., which has microfilmed directories for major cities to 1901.

Some of the best sources for biographical information are archives and manuscript collections. Pension records for military service are available in the National Archives and state archives, and are used regularly by genealogists and other researchers. The original federal census takers' enumeration forms contain information for most of the United States on individual households and, after 1850, on individuals. State and local governments often have pension records, tax lists, probate records, and other official records with biographical information. The *Guide to Genealogical Research in the National Archives* provides a good introduction to the use of federal records.

Authenticity

Researchers sometimes need to verify the authenticity of a written record. Most often, the researcher has discovered a letter or document signed by an important historical figure and wants to know whether it is genuine. Even though a letter bears the name of George Washington, is written on old paper, and was given to the archives fifty years ago by a prominent scholar, there is no guarantee that it is not a forgery, a hoax, or simply the work of another, historically unimportant, George Washington, misidentified as

President George Washington. Recently, at a flea market, a dealer showed a researcher an account book from the 1820s which included accounts with George Washington, the president. Very little effort is needed to establish that Washington has died more than twenty years previously. Yet a misidentification of this sort, often caused by wishful thinking, can be perpetuated in the collections of a historical society. There have been cases where published articles and books, purportedly based on original manuscripts, or copies of manuscripts, have been disproved or seriously questioned by scholars because of internal evidence in the documents. The article by Arthur T. Middleton and Douglass Adair on the Horn Papers in the *William and Mary Quarterly* in 1948, and John Y. Simon's 1983 article on the Margaret Johnson Erwin letters in the *Journal of American History* are examples of a critical approach to suspect historical documents. Leonard Rapport's "Fakes and Facsimiles: Problems of Identification," in the January 1979 issue of *American Archivist,* is useful not only for a brief introduction to authenticating documents, including widely reprinted copies of historical documents, but for insightful comments on the belief that a document is important in spite of evidence to the contrary.

The presumed signature of an important historical figure can be compared with examples in books used by autograph collectors. Charles Hamilton's *American Signatures* contains facsimile signatures of signers of the Declaration of Independence, Revolutionary War leaders, and United States presidents. Herbert Cahoon's *American Literary Autographs, from Washington Irving to Henry James* represents prominent literary figures. Mary Benjamin's *Autographs: A Key to Collecting,* the Manuscript Society's *Autographs and Manuscripts: A Collector's Manual* and several books by Charles Hamilton discuss signatures, forgeries, and mistaken identities.

However, not all copies of records are forgeries. There were many legitimate reasons for copying documents and letters. A Revolutionary War diary written on paper produced only after 1840 may have been a copy made for a family member or a historian. The original may now be lost or destroyed and the nineteenth-century copy may have itself become a valuable historical document. Although reference sources are useful, the researcher should be wary of establishing the authenticity of a letter through reference sources alone. Particularly when dealing with manuscript materials having monetary value, the best advice is to consult an expert.

PHILIP F. MOONEY

6. BUSINESS RECORDS

In addressing a topic as broad as business records, problems of definition quickly come to light. Both the ledger books maintained by a nineteenth-century artisan and the voluminous records generated by a contemporary Fortune 500 company document the functions of business enterprise, but collection of such materials has been sporadic and uneven. The agencies which traditionally collect historical materials have not placed a high priority on business records, preferring to focus on the records of institutions that have served the political, social, cultural, or religious needs of the community. In formulating their collecting canons, librarians and archivists have employed more restrictive standards for business records than for other types of material. Too often the criterion for preservation of business records has been the size of the collection rather than the content of the material or the economic importance of the institution.

On the other hand, American business itself has exhibited little concern for retention of historical materials, whether by an individual company or archival research centers. Of the thousands of business concerns that have flourished in the United States and have affected American society, only a small minority have recognized the value of the historical record and have taken steps to preserve it.

Part of the reason for corporate inattention to business records is the insular nature of business itself. Operating in an environment perceived to be antibusiness, most corporations reveal only that information which regulatory agencies require them to disclose or which has an obvious public relations benefit. The potentially devastating effects of adversarial litigation argue powerfully that the most prudent defensive posture is minimal documentation. In a corporate world characterized by fierce competition for market share, relatively few business concerns view their history as vital to operational success.

From an economic standpoint, history is costly and has a negative financial impact. One study suggests that American business produces an estimated 324 billion documents a year, and that an additional 72 billion documents are added each year. The average business letter costs over 6 dollars to produce and an additional 27 cents to file; maintenance of a standard four-drawer filing cabinet costs over 800 dollars per year in fixed costs, equipment, and salaries.[1] The cost of historical preservation is high, in spite of the typical archival retention rate of only 1 to 3 percent of corporate records and the economies achieved with bulk storage of materials. In terms of practical cost-justification, the shredder is often the preferred alternative.

This indifference to the future and its researchers has resulted in widely dispersed and often fragmentary collections with limited accessibility and rudimentary finding aids. The researcher attempting to identify, locate, and utilize business records will have to possess the persistence and ingenuity ascribed to the detective heroes of literature and television.

Despite this gloomy assessment of the overall state of American business documentation, a considerable body of material does exist in both the public and private sector. Virtually every historical society, manuscript repository, governmental archive, and university or public library special collections department has some material that is classified as business records. The real problem for the researcher is determining how various institutions have defined and interpreted such an ambiguous category. To the local historical society, geography is a primary determinant, while the antiquarian may look more favorably on documentation produced by early artisans and small merchants. Still other collections concentrate on themes such as transportation, agriculture, energy, motion pictures, ethnic enterprises, or publishing. Even governmental collections can yield valuable data through the records filed by regulatory bodies or by courts which preside over legal proceedings affecting business practice.

The very definition of corporate records has evolved over time to include broader categories of material. For many years, the standard business records were legal and financial documents that provided a capsule view of institutional activities. T. R. Schellenberg's classic volume on archival management presented the prevailing views of that time (1965), and focused narrowly on fiscal records such as cashbooks, ledgers, and journals, and their legal counterparts: decrees, decisions, judgments, articles of incorporation, and testaments.[2] Indeed, many older, established historical programs considered these to be the only records of value as research tools. For the researcher, the unfortunate result of this restrictive philosophy has often been one-dimensional collections which do not reflect the personality of the parent body.

For many years Harvard University was the only American institution to seriously collect "unprinted documents" relating to business. Focusing on the textile mills and manufacturing concerns of New England, Harvard recorded its first archival accession in 1916 and stimulated the formation of the Business History Society in 1925.[3] In the 1930s and 1940s, other academic institutions developed collections of primary sources in their libraries to support graduate research in business administration.[4] Corporations began to recognize the potential value of historical files, exemplified by the formation of internal archival collections at Firestone Tire and Rubber Company (1943), Insurance Company of North America (1944), Time, Inc. (1946), Armstrong Cork (1947), and Eastman Kodak (1949).[5] In the 1940s, the American Association of Museums published a study listing eighty companies which actively supported internal museums and maintained at least a basic historical collection.[6] From these roots, dozens of new corporate programs have developed to the point where the last published survey of business archives listed over two hundred programs in 1980,[7] and a recent study of corporate museums identified one hundred institutions that support visitors' centers, plant tours, and educational exhibits.[8]

This pattern of growth has placed history more prominently in the corporate spotlight. It reflects the expanded range of historical resources held by corporations. Most importantly for the researcher, it has institutionalized bodies of important corporate documentation and has helped to legitimize the historical function as an element in the business structure. The example set by Harvard has encouraged the development of other specialized business libraries, and most academic repositories have now acquired collections that treat economic or financial issues.

The scope of materials currently found in well-documented business collections extends far beyond the limited financial and legal parameters outlined by Schellenberg. Primary documentation often includes the minute books of corporations and committees of the board of directors; files of the president and key administrative officials; executives' speeches and research notes; strategic planning reports; articles of incorporation, contracts, agreements, mergers, litigation files and other major legal papers; shareholder lists and reports; departmental records; product histories; internal memoranda; tax and insurance records; journals, ledgers, budgets, and summary financial reports; advertising samples; marketing research data; photographs; sound recordings, film, and videotapes; and oral histories. A wealth of secondary source information exists in such repositories, including industry publications, press releases, printed marketing data, policy statements and official memoranda, newsletters, house organs, price lists, sales catalogs, annual and quarterly reports, pamphlets, corporate histories, handbills and ephemera, customer mailings, bulletins, manuals, official biographies, awards, scrapbooks, and photograph albums. In addition, many collections also include artifacts that range from valuable paintings and sculpture to advertising samples, packaging, awards, and memorabilia. These artifacts, which provide an opportunity for corporations to interpret their business activities to employees, clients, and the public, can be of great value to the researcher.

With this broad outline of resources in mind, the researcher can explore both the private and public sectors for pertinent materials. Standard reference works such as the *National Union Catalog of Manuscript Collections,* the *Directory of Archives and Manuscript Repositories in the United States,* published by the National Historical Publications and Records Commission, the new thirteenth edition of the *Directory of Historical Agencies in North America,* published by the American Association for State and Local History, and the *National Inventory of Documentary Sources in the United States* all provide a general overview of the field.[9] The subject indexes in these publications open up a wealth of materials that the researcher might not normally associate with the collections of major business information centers.

The extensive collections of such specialized institutions as the Baker Library at Harvard University; the Hagley Museum and Library in Wilmington, Delaware; the American Antiquarian Society in Worcester, Massachusetts; the Edison Institute at the Henry Ford Museum and Greenfield Village in Dearborn, Michigan; and the advertising history collections at the National Museum of American History in Washington, D.C., and the American Advertising Museum in Portland, Oregon, offer a wide variety of holdings to support the research of both amateur historian and serious scholar. These institutions encourage use of their materials by publicizing their holdings and employing trained subject specialists to guide the researcher through the maze of materials and assist in locating relevant items. In addition to collecting the primary resources found in the archives of major business enterprises, these centers actively acquire secondary materials (monographs, annual reports, pamphlets, photographs, trade catalogs, manuals, almanacs, and other printed items) too specialized for the general library. Many institutions have prepared detailed finding aids to their collections that are readily available to researchers on request;[10] others have issued brochures or guides to introduce researchers to the breadth of their holdings. All are equipped to handle telephone and letter requests on a timely basis.

A final area which should not be overlooked by the researcher into business records is oral history. Almost every major public or private institution in America holds oral records in one form or another. Collections of oral history recordings have multiplied over the last two decades as large and small repositories have seen the potential of capturing information not documented in any other fashion. While the quality and value of some of these programs is open to question, many subjects related to business history have been captured. Whether the tapes focus on a specific enterprise, like the Dr. Pepper Company collection at Baylor University, or deal with a specific element in the corporate structure, like the oral history advertising collections on Alka-Seltzer, Marlboro cigarettes, and Pepsi-Cola at the Smithsonian Institution, they foster understanding of how modern corporations function. The researcher should note that oral history tapes may have indirect references to business information that only become apparent through close scrutiny of the available finding aids and discussion with the staff of the information center.

When the researcher turns from public institutions and attempts to secure information directly from the private sector, the quest becomes more difficult. Corporate sources present roadblocks and restrictions that can hinder anyone and frustrate the uninformed. While basic historical information is usually available from corporations, researchers seeking direct access to company records may encounter significant difficulty. A letter or telephone call directed to the public relations department or the office of the corporate secretary generally will yield whatever public information is available. Consumer information departments and community or public affairs offices may provide similar or related information. Current annual reports, historical brochures, and other materials reflective of corporate operations can often be obtained without charge or at nominal cost. Bibliographies and references to other works about the company may also be available. Although the quality of such publications varies widely, most share the common characteristic of in-house authorship, a text reflecting the historical perspective of management written in a positive and upbeat style.[11] Occasionally corporations contract with historians or allow independent researchers access to company files in order to produce a work which presents an impartial, outsider view of the firm. These endeavors have often resulted in worthwhile books that provide a balanced view of corporate development.[12]

Other sources of historical information exist within corporate walls, but access to them is difficult. Even though at least two hundred American corporations support in-house archival programs, they serve the internal reference needs of the company and offer very limited access to the researcher. In the vast majority of cases, a corporate archives operates with a small staff and limited budget, and a high priority is placed on the archivist's ability to supply executives with data quickly and efficiently. Public relations, security, legal, and competitive concerns make many firms reluctant to open their files to outsiders. If there is no clear benefit to the company, the usual policy is to keep information resources centralized and unavailable.

Among major corporations maintaining archival collections are consumer-goods companies (Coca-Cola, Sears, Procter and Gamble, Domino's Pizza, Kraft, Anheuser-Busch, Weyerhaeuser, Corning, General Mills, and Walt Disney); financial institutions (Chase Manhattan, New York Stock Exchange, Wells Fargo, Nationwide Insurance, Bank of America, and Cigna); high technology industries (United Technologies, Control Data, and Texas Instruments), communications firms (American Telephone and Telegraph, ITT); advertising agencies (J. Walter Thompson, N. W. Ayer); transportation companies (John Deere, International Harvester, and Boeing), and institutions which do not fit into an easily definable category such as Colonial Williamsburg, Educational Testing Service, and New England Medical Center.

Funding is provided for an archival program when a company determines that a centralized source for historical records has positive benefits. As a staff service, the archives primarily supports the following areas of the business: marketing, public relations, legal, personnel, advertising, training, strategic planning, publications, research and development, shareholder relations, merchandise licensing, and financial. By providing a historical perspective for company operations, the archives can help to generate positive public relations programs and to support corporate decision making.

With a mandate to serve internal company needs, few corporate archives allow unrestricted access to their holdings. Many prohibit outside researchers entirely, while others set up lengthy waiting periods before files can be opened. Institutions frequently restrict the outside researcher to material which is at least twenty-five years old. Other archives allow noncompany personnel to have access only to public documents generated by the corporation, such as press releases, advertising executions, published financial data, photographs, company publications, and speeches. The company archivist may insist on formally scheduled appointments and screening interviews before materials are made available to an outsider. In all cases, corporate collections are private collections, and access is at the discretion of the institution. Researchers who understand the nature of such collections and who are willing to be flexible in dealing with the idiosyncrasies of the corporate environment have a much better chance of receiving help than those who do not.

Even when access is granted, researchers are sometimes disappointed with the quality of the finding aids available. Because of the volume of records handled in a corporate archives and the need to establish some preliminary control over the records, the initial accession record, with its quick summation of content, may be the only information available on a collection for months or even years after it has been received. Unlike collections in academic institutions that processors describe in detail to bring out all possible research topics, corporate collections rarely achieve that level of description where records are grouped by type (e.g., correspondence, speeches, subject files). It is the archivist's knowledge of the materials (supported by at least minimal indexing) that provides accessibility to materials in the collection. Outside researchers should anticipate extended time requirements for locating specific documents, which may have to be reviewed carefully one at a time to find particular items of information.

While the archives is the ideal organizational unit to preserve and reference historical information, it is not the only place in which corporate America stores its heritage. Many corporations which cannot justify the expense of maintaining an archival program designate other units to perform this function. Most often, the records management program, public relations department, or corporate library assumes maintenance of historical documentation by executive mandate or default. Researchers should be aware of these possibilities. However, because documenting historical activity is a secondary responsibility in these departments, the researcher is less likely to receive encouragement there or even to gain access. Patience and understanding are key qualities for the researcher who hopes to have access to corporate materials. A corporation which has submerged its historical documentation within an organizational unit other than the archives or library has made a statement about the value of history to its business, and it is unlikely that there will be much interest in the researcher whose perception of the value of such documentation differs.

The significant and accessible body of material which will support a business-oriented researcher is to be found in public institutions. This situation will undoubtedly continue because there is little movement in the private sector toward opening files to interested researchers, and the growth rate for new business record-keeping programs has remained unchanged in the last five years. Even within the public sector, there is unlikely to be much growth in the number of collections made available to the public. Present-day budgetary constraints on public repositories have curbed interest in acquiring extensive corporate collections with high processing and maintenance costs. Corporate policy weighs against free access to business collections, and researchers who need such material often must fight to change institutional perceptions and policy in order to have their needs even partially met.

ENID T. THOMPSON

7.   RELIGIOUS RECORDS

Church and religious records are among the oldest records to be created and preserved throughout the world. They appear among almost every people, and in nearly every area, culture, and language. The clan and the religious institution were the first social organizations. Feeling a need for order, for understanding the past, and for information about individuals, they created records by various available means: pictographs, artifacts, and words. They were first in the oral tradition, and ultimately in writing. Religions have known, stable personnel and defined territories; they are respected and their records have been regularly protected, used, and studied.

In the early Christian church, the development of record keeping was encouraged by common language, central administrative organization, and unified governance. Many present-day record-keeping practices are outgrowths of these early beginnings. Today's legal jurisdictions accept religious records as evidentiary, an example of how a long and consistent history contributes to evidence. Without the documentation of religious history, there would be a lamentable lack of documentation for long stretches of human experience.

Religious records are a rich source for researchers in local and regional history. The reason is readily apparent: religion has been central to both community and personal life in any society. Religious records deal with realities common to the group and important to the individual; they identify community norms and they delineate personal history, such as births, marriages, deaths, and other rites of passage. Priests, the primary record keepers, were often the only literate persons in a community. The church in the Western world early recognized the need for records and record keepers.

Current dictionaries still identify a clerk as a record keeper or a clergyman. Originally a clerk was anyone who could read or write, and the church educated its clergy so that they could read and keep the required records.

As Christianity spread, most of the happenings of everyday life were recorded by priests who were required to register births, marriages, deaths, and relationship and kinship records. The church dealt with everyone from ruler to illegitimate peasant-beggar on a person-to-person basis; little escaped its eye or its pen. As long as a church building has survived, researchers can presume unbroken custody, in the hands of successive parish priests, of records covering centuries of individual lives and community disasters and other events. Consequently, church records are constantly used for research by historians, genealogists, sociologists, and family members.

The types of records kept by churches, usually on a parish level and retained in the parish, include:

> membership lists
> births and observances celebrating the naming of children
> marriages
> deaths and burials
> parish school records
> financial records
> minutes of meetings to conduct parish business
> church group activities
> architectural records of construction and repair
> sermons
> newsletters, bulletins, and other ephemera

If a religious congregation is part of a larger governing body, such as a diocese or synod, the governing body may keep these records at its headquarters or other central repository, but most denominations retain parish records in the home locality. Local clergy can often assist researchers in finding information.

Marriage, birth, and death records are especially important to religious groups, and the record in an official register (with its attendant certificate) of a marriage, baptism, circumcision, or burial is considered legally evidentiary, if an organized denomination has kept its records archivally. This means that events have been recorded in chronological order by the responsible officer and the records maintained in unbroken custody by succeeding officers, priests, ministers, or rabbis. The usual method of recording is to use a sturdily bound registry book with numbered pages. The information is basic: who, what, when, where, how, and occasionally why. The names of the principals involved, witnesses, place, date, and activity are listed, often with signatures. The certificate issued to the principals is usually numbered to make the record in the register easier to find, although it can be found without a number. The date of the event is another way to search. Marriage, death, and christening registers are especially valuable to genealogical researchers, who sometimes can supplement burial records with information from a gravestone in the adjacent churchyard.

Minutes of church meetings are not always as accessible to researchers as registers. Files of newsletters and bulletins sometimes exist, and the researcher must inquire of the local priest, minister, or rabbi. Access to congregational records is secured by writing or visiting the appropriate incumbent clergyman to present the researcher's reasons for seeking information. If the congregational records have been removed to a central repository, the clergyman can direct the researcher.

The Church of Jesus Christ of Latter-Day Saints, commonly called the Mormon Church, has a particularly strong interest in genealogy and church records. For many years the Mormons have collected religious records (non-Mormon as well as Mormon,) from virtually all over the world on microfilm or in book form. Arranged by nation of origin, the records are available to Mormon and non-Mormon researchers in the Genealogical Library of the Church in Salt Lake City, Utah, and in the branch libraries that the Mormons have established throughout the United States. (The branch libraries can be located by looking for Church of Christ of Latter-Day Saints under *Churches* in the yellow pages of the telephone book.) Although material not in the branch libraries can be obtained for branch use from the main library in Salt Lake City, the researcher will find a visit to the main library with its easily accessible holdings very rewarding.

A starting place for researchers seeking religious records is the library in a nearby seminary or other institution offering a religious studies program. Even if the library is not one maintained by the denomination of concern, there will be good general research tools, and the librarians will probably be acquainted with other collections and subject specialists. They can be especially good guides to local religious records.

ENID T. THOMPSON

8. PUBLIC RECORDS

Public records are documents created and preserved by a government agency in the conduct of its business. Records can originate from nations, states, counties, cities, villages, townships, departments, or subdivisions of any of these. Public records cover every aspect of governmental activity from foreign policy to the transactions of dog wardens. Kept in the custody of the officer who created them, they are subsequently turned over to his successor. In territories less extensive than a state, the usual officer of record is the county or city clerk.

Managing the wealth of records in a jurisdiction is a major responsibility. To maintain its records, the United States government requires a large skilled staff and extensive storage space in the National Archives, eleven regional archives and records centers, and a growing number of presidential libraries. Each state has (or needs) an archives; the state archives is often an independent agency, although it may be a department of the state library, history center, or museum. All states have or are presently developing public records offices.[1]

A beginning researcher locates public records offices through historical societies and county clerks or other local administrative officers. The researcher must remember that public records were created by a branch of government to assist in carrying out its business. The use of records by researchers is almost always a secondary purpose for a public records collection.

Title to public records belongs absolutely to the agency which created them. The records are housed in the office of origin until it can no longer maintain them, when they are sent to the records center or archives established to receive them. The official who created them has no legal right to take them when he leaves office.

Records thus removed are said to be "alienated," and most states have passed laws of replevin to protect against loss of their records in this way. *Replevin* is the legal process by which the proper office or archive can recover papers and place them in the appropriate record group or repository.

Each county, city, and village has its clerk and records office. In 1980 there were 81,000 repositories of records in the United States;[2] each was developed to serve a purpose, and local governments cannot function without them. However, since records are indigenous to the area which produced them, there are many variations, not only in the records themselves, but in where they are kept and how they are serviced. Direct inquiry to state historical societies, county clerks, and agency officers is the method by which a researcher learns of and gains access to public records.

Archival practice postulates the methods of arranging and describing public records. The records group is determined and identified by the office of origin and the administrative function of the records. Records are arranged chronologically in the order of creation. This is the archival principle of original order—*respect des fonds*.

To aid in finding materials, a records management system is instituted. When records are created, as in the case of property records in a clerk's office or incorporation records in a state archives, each is numbered, and like records are kept together. An index listing record numbers is created to provide easy retrieval of a desired record from the file. In early record keeping, the index records were entered numerically in a book called a register, and registered records had legal standing. Today entries are largely computer-generated and stored.

Public records are arranged in archives according to the groups in which the records were created, and for easier control, the groups are divided into subgroups: series, subseries, file. If the records are correspondence files or other bulky series, rather than individual items, they are inventoried and rarely indexed. An inventory usually lists only the subjects of series and personal names. The inventory describes the contents briefly (quantity, persons named, dates, and subjects) and indicates the location of the desired papers. The appropriate file or document is usually then found, by the researcher.

Another important archival principle is that of unbroken custody. This means that the original documents remain permanently
in the continuous custody of the proper officer or his designated
replacement, the archivist. There can be no deviation from this
principle; the line of custody must be unbroken and provable to
establish provenance. Unbroken custody is often proved by num-
bering each document sequentially as it is created. This facilitates
finding individual documents because each document can be inventoried or indexed by number. (This is a variant of the register
system, the oldest of all archival systems.)

Property records are numbered, registered, and usually microfilmed in numerical order for research use, but they must first be
looked up in notoriously large and heavy ledgers in the office of
the county or city clerk. Property records include deeds, liens,
grantor or grantee records, transfers of title, mortgages, and tax
records, all extremely important because they must be traced with
all transfers of property. The various documents are not considered
property records until they have been recorded and assigned a
number by the clerk. The date on which the notarized document
was assigned a number and entered into the clerk's ledger is the
date of record. The record, or an attested copy of it, remains in the
clerk's office in perpetuity where anyone can inspect it.

Although the principles cited above cover public records in any
repository from the National Archives to the offices of county,
city, court, and even church clerks, a researcher must determine
which repository has the desired records. Help is available from
librarians, archivists, and clerks who are adept at using finding aids
and knowledgeable about the repositories and collections in their
area. They can direct a researcher to the proper source and save
research time. Librarians and archivists are also skilled at asking
questions to focus on what material is really required. There is
sometimes a difference between what the researcher thinks he
wants and what he really needs.

In dealing with a question which has involved the United States
government, such as a federal court decision or a subject falling
within the province of a federal department, the researcher should
approach the nearest branch of the National Archives and Records
Administration (NARA). NARA archivists can indicate where such

varied items as Indian tribal records, military records, water papers, and court cases are to be found. These records are often deposited in the geographical area where they were created, but, if not, an NARA branch can often borrow them from Washington.

Perhaps the resource most used at any NARA regional center is the census of the United States. Available to anyone, public demand occasionally necessitates a time limit on use because the census is on microfilm and must be read on a reader. Printed copies of each page may be purchased.

The population census is taken in the "zero" year of each decade. The first national census was undertaken in 1790, a simple listing of the number of people living in a state, to assure equitable congressional representation. As early as 1810, the census began to elicit more information, and currently the Bureau of the Census gathers and publishes much information dealing with population distribution and composition, agriculture, business and manufacturing, natural resources, housing, incomes, and other demographic facts.

The United States population census is a listing of persons by name, age, address, sex, place of birth, naturalization, occupation, income, education, and details of housing down to the number of bathrooms in one's home. Because census questions occasionally involve personal information, a census is not made entirely public until 72 years after its gathering. The 1910 census was made public in 1982, just as the 1920 census will be placed in repositories in 1992. There is one unfortunate exception: the 1890 census records were burned and are not available at all.

The detailed index to the personal names in the census is called the Soundex. Many libraries that do not have copies of the census have copies of the Soundex to enable researchers to find out whether the person they seek is in the census. The Soundex for the 1920 census is the most recent one available.

Several states have undertaken census lists of their own, usually in a year between the decennial dates of the federal census. For example, the Colorado census of 1885 greatly helps researchers working on the period for which federal census records are not available. The loss of the 1890 census can be partially overcome; for information dealing with a particular geographical region, the researcher should consult an archivist or librarian in the area.

The archives of a state, like those of the nation, reflect the organization of the state government and are arranged according to three principal functions: executive, legislative, and judicial. Occasionally groups or series of records are closed or restricted, and early papers may have been alienated or are estranged. The words *alienated, estranged,* and *estrayed,* are often used in referring to records which have disappeared. *Alienated* implies that the records were deliberately removed, as by a former officeholder; *estranged* means lost or unclaimed; *estrayed* usually implies that they disappeared along with their records group. The words are sometimes used interchangeably. Restricted records, if available, are kept in archives, usually on microfilm, unless they have been kept in the office of origin.

Vital statistics are usually kept in the state health department. Copies of birth and death certificates are not issued without identification and a valid reason for viewing them. Adoption records are usually sealed, although in recent years there have been lawsuits to open them. Other state records remain in the agency that created them, e.g., prison records in the corrections department and mining records in the department of mines. The state archives staff can direct researchers to these locations.

Local public records are neither as structured nor as uniform as federal and state records.[3] They vary widely from state to state, region to region, and jurisdiction to jurisdiction. Created by local government agencies primarily for administrative use, they contain a tremendous wealth of information about local conditions, people, and history. As Thomas E. Felt says,

> You may not know much about government, but your government has always known a lot about you and your ancestors. All the highlights and turns of fortune in life have long been recorded somewhere in the official records: birth, death, taxes, inheritances, licenses, marriage and divorce, property transfers, bankruptcies and lawsuits.[4]

The traditional functions of local government are upholding peace and order, and maintaining laws and courts, roads, and schools. Because money is needed to finance these activities, public records are developed from the assessment, collection, and expenditure of public funds. Once undertaken, the process never ends.

The governmental organization and activities of each region reflect its own needs, customs, and background. In the early period of settlement, isolation and difficulty in communication led to distinctive practices. Both government and record keeping still have strong local overtones, and national and state archives have had little influence upon them. Because of a comparatively late start and the need to organize an enormous accumulation of state and national records, the larger collections could not arbitrarily insist upon similar standards throughout the country. Only now are records managers and archivists beginning to receive standardized training. It is no wonder that a religiously funded New England township, a slaveholding county in the deep South, a rowdy mining camp in the far West, and a Scandinavian agricultural community in the Midwest still show differences in record keeping today.

The researcher needing local records must ask at state and local historical society libraries and archives, and at offices of county and city clerks and county court clerks. The trail of local records may lead to the assessor's office, the water board, or the attic of the courthouse.

Public records most used by researchers fall into the following categories:

Vital statistics. Records not in the custody of the state are probably in the office of the county clerk. Birth and death records are usually kept by the state. Marriage licenses are issued by the county clerk. Divorce records are maintained by the courts.

Property. Although the records are kept in the office of the city or county clerk, they are indexed by address in the assessor's office.

Taxes. Records are generally privileged or sealed. They are housed in the office of the county clerk or county treasurer.

Military and veterans. Records are usually kept by the state, although military records are sometimes maintained by local militia groups.

Naturalization. Records are held by the district court.

School. Records are kept in the school district office or by the county clerk. Sometimes school records are in the state archives, but if so, they are often estranged.

Inquests. Records are kept in the coroner's office or by the county clerk.

Orphans, apprentices, and the disadvantaged. Records may be in the offices of the health department, social services department, or county clerk.

Transportation. Records dealing with roads, mass transit, ferry systems, bridges, and river transport are housed in the state or county transportation office or in the county clerk's office.

Planning and zoning. Records are kept by the planning department or by the city or county clerk.

Wills and estates. Records are maintained by the clerk of the probate court.

Trial courts and grand juries. Although usually kept by the court clerk, records are sometimes in the state archives.

Power of attorney. Records are kept by the county or court clerk.

Business licenses, permits, etc. Records are filed with the city or county clerk. Incorporation records are kept by the Secretary of State.

Maps, plats, streets. Records are kept by the city or county clerk.

All of the above records and their repositories reflect the local area and its development. A law court was usually the first legal organization established, and in most cases, a church was the first social organization. This means that birth, death, and marriage records can be either religious or civil. Land records were established almost as early because property ownership and definition must be registered in order to be defensible. From early in United States history, the agency of record was a court, whether organized by town, township, county, city, or territory, and the clerk of the court was the recorder. The earliest court records covered all functions: property ownership, marriages, inquests of deaths, etc. In areas where the public assumed responsibility for the general education of the young, school records also began early. They were, and often still are, the responsibility of the clerk of the school board.

The costs of courts, land offices, and schools necessitated money, which came from assessments and various taxes based upon land holdings, a head count, privileges such as use of roads, wood collecting, or any other activity that the locality chose. The taxes in turn created new records that had to be kept in perpetuity.

Social problems and care for the needy produced public records of orphans, apprentices, paupers, and other disadvantaged wards of the public. Birth, death, marriage, adoption, and divorce became matters for the public record. Wills had to be probated; the courts kept copies of wills and records of administration of estates. Civil and criminal lawsuits were recorded. Election records were filed. Military service records, which began with the militia at the time of the French and Indian War, soon included veterans' records. Immigration and naturalization records developed as foreign-born persons arrived and became United States citizens. Transportation records came into being as roads and bridges were built and repaired, tolls collected, and transit systems created.

Investigative records grew with the development of police, grand juries, and political activity. Maintained by the jurisdiction responsible for the investigation, access is secured through the clerk of the court or the city or county clerk. Inquest records are kept by the county coroner.

Public records of businesses vary as to office of record. Records of active companies, except for licenses and permits, articles of incorporation, liens, and annual reports, are maintained by the individual firm. Licenses and permits are recorded by county or city clerks; incorporation papers, liens, and annual reports are recorded by the Secretary of State within each state. Records of defunct corporations are in the state archives. The county clerk usually maintains records of property, tax payments, and liens outstanding, but mortgage foreclosures are recorded in the court which handled them.

Different areas of the country have specialized types of records.

Examples are the maritime records of coastal areas and the water records of the arid West where there are special water courts. Researchers in various repositories, records centers, archives, and libraries must ask many questions to discover the range of local records.

Most local jurisdictions are now struggling with the continuous proliferation of records. As a result of the deluge, records managers may be driven to dispose of more records than they know to be advisable. Although it is a basic principle of records management that not all records are of sufficient evidentiary or historical value to merit archival processing and service, this fact occasionally works against the preservation of local records. As an example, there is the disappearance of the abstract as a property record and its replacement by title insurance. An abstract listed every transaction concerning a piece of property with date and history. Grants, title changes, liens, restrictions, covenants, rights, and any other legal records were included. Title insurance merely states that the title has been searched and is insured in case of lawsuits against it.

The quantity of records now being produced has necessitated new methods of record keeping that reduce the bulk of ledgers and papers. Today, when local records are microfilmed or entered into a computer, originals are often destroyed, although the permanence of film, tapes, or disks has not been sufficiently tested by time to duplicate the preservation qualities of a well-bound ledger.

Local records may be sealed to protect privary. Tax records, adoption records, and some court records are regularly sealed. In many cases, departments of vital statistics will not issue copies of death certificates to persons who are not related to the decedent. Researchers will find that restrictions of local records vary greatly, from state archives to offices of county clerks.

JUDITH ANN SCHIFF

9. NONMANUSCRIPT SOURCES

Iconographic Sources

Photographs, stereographs, and postcards provide documentation to supplement manuscript records; they sometimes constitute the only surviving information on a research subject. Unfortunately, some researchers ignore the value of photographic materials, utilizing it for illustrative purposes only. Many historians have eschewed photographs as a serious source of information. Some historians admit their historical value, but state that they are much more difficult to interpret than written records. Other researchers frankly confess that they do not know how to "read" photographs. Older historiographical handbooks generally do not provide guidance on the use of photographs as historical evidence.

In the past, researchers distrusted photographs when written documentation was available, believing the written word to be more trustworthy. While it is true that photographs can distort evidence, the written record may also contain distortions. Researchers who view a photograph as a historical record can ask the same questions they would ask about a manuscript: identification of the author and recipient, format, subject, and relationship to a group of records.

Effective examination of historical photographs depends upon their arrangement and description in the archives center. In some repositories, pictorial material is separated from the main collection of papers and housed in a picture collection which may be in another department or building. Photographs left with the papers to which they relate often are not inventoried or cross-indexed. The researcher who wishes to examine photographs must develop a good research strategy with the assistance of the archivist and be willing to devote time to both searching for and studying them.

Once potentially relevant photographs have been located, they must be examined slowly and carefully, in association with extant related written records. Often they must be reviewed and reevaluated several times before their full evidential historical value is revealed. For example, a photograph of a cluttered college dormitory room taken in 1890 will provide data on educational history, smoking and drinking, music and theatre history, food, clothing, sports, heating and lighting, furnishings, and other aspects of social history.

Photographic history begins in 1839 with the introduction of daguerreotypes and paper prints. At first the paper print did not gain widespread acceptance, and the daguerreotype was the more popular type of photography until the mid-1850s. The daguerreotype is a one-of-a-kind photograph produced directly on a silver-coated copper plate without a negative. Its mirrorlike appearance distinguishes it from other unique photographs, such as the ambrotype and the tintype. The ambrotype, which was developed in the 1850s, was less expensive to produce. Each ambrotype was a negative developed on the back of a glass plate; when the negative image was coated with black varnish, it appeared as a positive image from the other side of the glass. The tintype was the least expensive form of single print, remaining in popular use until the early part of the twentieth century. It is easily recognized by its darker appearance and thin iron plate. As paper prints improved in quality, their ability to be produced in multiple copies without a glaring surface put them in command of the market by the late 1850s.

To make effective use of photographs, the researcher should become familiar with the outline of photographic history and learn to identify the basic types of prints and negatives. This is especially important when assigning dates to undated photographs. Early paper prints prior to 1860 were mainly calotypes or salt prints characterized by a mat finish in sepia tones which tend to fade. They were superseded by albumen prints which had a semiglossy appearance and fine surface image. Albumen prints became universal and remained popular until about 1890. Toward the end of the nineteenth century, many advances in photographic technology were introduced, including platinum prints, characterized by very fine gray tones; gum bichromates, used for artistic, soft-focus prints; cyanotypes, blue-toned prints seen in family albums up to World War I; celluloid roll film which enabled amateurs to take their own snapshots; and emulsion papers.

Stereographs enjoyed two periods of great popularity, from their introduction in the early 1850s until the 1870s, and from the late 1880s until motion picture theatres became widespread in the twentieth century. Also known as stereoscope cards or stereo views, stereographs are twin photographs which create a three-dimensional effect when viewed through the eyepieces of a stereoscope. This effect is achieved from viewing two photographs of the same subject, each taken from a slightly different angle. Millions of stereographs were produced for educational and entertainment purposes. From the mid-nineteenth through the early twentieth centures, they provided documentation of famous landmarks and personalities, foreign travel, and local scenes and customs.

Postcards utilize both photographic and printed graphic images. Virtually every United States town and village had postcards for sale; they often provide the only extant pictorial record of communities, showing changes in specific sites over time. Millions of postcards have survived because of their popularity as souvenirs and because the "penny postcard" was the most convenient and economical form of communication for many years. When young Charles Lindbergh drove from Minnesota to California with his mother in 1916, he collected postcards from almost every town through which they passed. His collection of several hundred postcards provides an excellent documentation of small-town western America just before World War I. The history of transportation, for instance, is depicted on a card showing the contemporaneous utilization of the horse, the automobile, and the trolley, as well as displaying the dismal state of the national road system.

Graphic material such as posters, prints, letterheads, and other printed collectible items is often abundant in archival collections. Like other types of nonmanuscript items, graphic material is usually not individually cataloged or indexed. The historical evidence in printed pictorial material can also prove to be invaluable, especially in items that predate photography. Letterheads and billheads carry rare images of factories, offices, and business and career activities. Examples are a massive turn-of-the-century rubber goods factory with its many smokestacks belching black funnel clouds into the air and the hand-painted radium dials featured on the printed letterhead of a watch company.

More recent archival collections may include slides, motion picture films, recordings, and videotapes. Changes in technology and format have made it difficult or impossible to project and play some of this material in an archives center. The deterioration of many early films and recordings threatens their continued existence. Most 35 millimeter film, whether motion picture or early microfilm, is nitrate-based and a serious fire hazard. Researchers who may not currently be permitted to utilize resources because of their fragility should understand the need for the restrictions which archives have been forced to place on them. When such resources are accessible, the researcher must handle them with extreme care to conserve them for other users.

In the course of working on a subject, a researcher sometimes creates or acquires pictorial source material which would augment the archival collection. As an example, in interviewing the subject of a biographical study, the researcher may take photographs of the subject's home or artifacts. After the researcher has used the material, it would be appropriate to offer it to the archives center to preserve a pictorial record that might be lost to future researchers.

Ephemera

Ephemera refers to disposable informational literature. A feature of modern society, its forms include promotional handouts, fliers, paper placemats, political handbills, and programs. Ephemera is intended to last only briefly, and most of it easily disappears from our lives, tossed out as trash or dropped in the streets as litter. Usually created to serve a single purpose, such as notification of a meeting, motivation to vote for a political candidate, or advertisement of a product, ephemera appears to be something to discard after a short life of usefulness. It sometimes seems that a torrent of newly generated ephemera is threatening to drown us, and that it is impossible to curtail its production. Yet looking over ephemera of the past elicits a very different response. For example, a collection of eighteenth-century broadside cartoons or poems can call forth a feeling of nostalgia, a close historical presence, and a sensitized appreciation of value.

Today, cultural researchers, sociologists, art historians, and other subject specialists are becoming increasingly interested in ephemera as material culture, artifacts, and documents of history. The historical importance of a handbill advertising a women's suffrage meeting in 1917 is readily recognized. There is similar value, for a public-health study, of a brochure printed in 1919 advertising the "Dental AutoXray Unit," described and illustrated as a simple unit which provided rays for "one to ten seconds as you desire" without any protective lead apron, and was designed to operate "for years without attention."

Ephemera often turns up in manuscript collections. Usually retained by archivists, it may sometimes be difficult to locate. In larger historical societies, printed ephemera may be separated from the manuscript collection and placed in special collections of political handbills or broadsides. Other repositories may leave ephemera with the manuscript collection but house them in a "miscellaneous" box without a description of the series. Researchers may have to spend long periods searching for the items they seek. A railroad historian or collector of railroad timetables must be willing to search not only railroad company records, but the miscellaneous memorabilia file in a collection of family papers which may include a few timetables saved from a long-ago trip.

Family historians can uncover many facets of their ancestors' lives by carefully studying family ephemera. Memorabilia of special events, as well as of everyday life, can be found in scrapbooks or diaries and commonplace books. Details spanning decades of twentieth-century life are evoked in a handful of family souvenirs containing a handbill of the Bull Moose Party, four speakeasy cards (including one that actually reads "Joe sent me"), several unused World War II gasoline- and meat-ration stamps, and a flier giving directions to a Washington peace march.

A few far-sighted historians have created special collections of ephemera which they have donated to archival repositories. Archivists are also forming collections of ephemera, often by picking up literature and encouraging others to join in documenting protest movements or local events. Collecting specialized ephemera is an entertaining, educational hobby, which can prove to be a valuable historical resource. In the late 1930s, a Yale University professor became fascinated by the 1933 Century of Progress Exposition in Chicago and by the 1939 New York World's Fair. He viewed the earlier fair as a hundred-year survey of American history and the latter as a combination of state-of-the-art technology and dreams of the future. The professor wrote to the administrators of the expositions and to all of the exhibitors, requesting copies of all publications and handouts. Abundant material was sent, including product brochures, stickers, pins, photographs, menus, and educational literature. The material was organized, filed in steel cabinets, and deposited in the Yale library. The professor predicted that fifty years later historians would find the collection an invaluable resource. Years passed, and the dusty file cabinets were forgotten in the upper reaches of the library stacks. In the late 1970s when preparations began for the fortieth anniversary of the New York World's Fair, the file cabinets were discovered, turned over to the manuscripts department, and archivally processed. The prediction of the historian proved to be accurate; the collection has been frequently examined and utilized by researchers of all kinds: social historians, art and architecture scholars, students, "world's fair" enthusiasts, and collectors.

Another special collection of ephemera at Yale has yet to demonstrate its archival value. During 1976, the United States Bicentennial, Jesse Lemish, a social historian, compiled an art exhibit of give-away graphic materials and souvenirs, entitled "Bibliographic Schlock." The collection has been stored, unused, in the vault at Yale to await the test of historical time and interest.

Newspapers, Regional Novels, and Poetry

Brief mention should be made of collections of printed material maintained by repositories to support their manuscript collections. These published materials should not be overlooked by the researcher. Local newspapers, privately printed family and town histories, and regional novels and poetry supplement archival records. Often they may not be available elsewhere. The personal viewpoints expressed in poetry, humor, and fiction, as well as in newspaper features and memorial tributes, provide background for a fuller understanding of the manuscript records. In addition to filling factual gaps and fleshing out characters, local publications can substantiate (or discredit) the validity of subjective statements in personal papers.

WILLA K. BAUM AND BONNIE HARDWICK

10. ORAL HISTORIES

The historian of mid-twentieth-century America will not find the
abundance of letters, diaries, memos, telegrams, and personal
written materials that enliven and guide research of an earlier
period. Important decisions are made in face-to-face conferences
or by telephone, while a mountain of machine-produced paper-
work threatens to bury even the trail of the events resulting from
those verbal interchanges. There is too much paper, too little
substance. However, technology has come to the rescue with a
means of recording the personal accounts of the movers and shakers
of the age and, even more particularly, the accounts of those who
have been moved or shaken. That recording is called oral history.

Oral history is the many voices of the people—every segment of
the people—recollecting historical events or movements which have
taken place in their time and within their view. For the researcher
these voices bring the excitement of the struggle to the dry formal
account of events, provide the missing clues about why tables were
suddenly turned, and form the human link between researchers of
today and the everyday life of the past. They are voices that can
guide the researcher through countless linear feet of manuscript
boxes.

The narrator may be a governor, a Supreme Court justice, a coal
miner, a Dust Bowl migrant to California, a Japanese-American
internee, a World War II defense plant worker, or a recent Southeast
Asian immigrant. The narrators may talk about their localities,
occupations, ethnic groups, participation in an event—anything in
their own lives (and those of their forebears who shaped the
present) from childhood to old age. In each case the result is a
vivid, often poignant, and always personal window on the past.

This chapter is devoted to methods of finding already produced archival oral histories which are available for research. If there is no existing archival oral history relating to a researcher's topic of investigation, the reseacher may wish to pursue the creation of an oral history. Some manuals on how to undertake oral history production are listed in the bibliography for this chapter.

Before getting into the uneasy territory of finding and using oral history, a definition of oral history and its various forms is in order. The Oral History Association, in its *Oral History Evaluation Guidelines,* defines exemplary oral history as tape-recorded interviews with persons selected for their personal knowledge of historically significant events or ways of life. The guidelines specify that interviews are in question-and-answer form, guided by a skilled and knowledgeable interviewer. The resulting interviews have been reviewed by both interviewer and interviewee to verify that the statements are as accurate as possible. If not quite in the class of legal depositions, they are nonetheless carefully planned and verified accounts, not spontaneous conversations which are better suited, perhaps, for a folklore collection. Oral history interviews are open for historical research in a repository, and the interviewer and interviewee have signed a release indicating that others may read and quote from the materials.

An exemplary oral history is available in transcript form, corrected and verified by the narrator, with the interview tapes available for listening. An introductory interview explains the reason for the oral history and the circumstances of its recording. The transcript is indexed for quick location of names and subjects; photographs, copies of important supporting materials, and miscellaneous papers are also on file. This "ideal" oral history may also be part of a series which presents diverse viewpoints on the same topic.

In actuality, many oral histories may be less perfect. At worst, there may be bundles of tapes identified only by name of narrator and date of interview, with no description of the purpose or circumstances of the recording nor any guides to the contents. If the researcher is more fortunate, there will be a descriptive log of the contents of each tape, an indication of time segments, and an explanation of the purpose of the oral histories. There may, however, be a mixture of tapes and partial transcripts, with or without proper releases permitting use of the material for research and publication.

Besides oral histories, libraries collect other kinds of sound recordings which are useful to the history researcher, such as recordings of speeches, city council meetings, professional meetings, radio and television broadcasts, folklore recordings, and historic "documents" like the Watergate tapes. These are *sound recordings,* not *oral history,* because they were not created specifically and purposely for historical research and they have not been verified by the narrator. Nevertheless, both oral histories and sound recordings can add information and sparkle to historical research.

The invention of the tape recorder in the late 1940s made oral history possible. The popularization of cassette tape recorders has brought recording equipment within the price range and technical capability of almost any historical group or individual researcher. A decade ago the United States bicentennial celebration helped raise community consciousness about the value of individual accounts. Thousands of organizations in the United States are, or recently have been, engaged in some kind of oral history project. The groups range from high schools, community museums and libraries, historical societies, and colleges and universities, to religious institutions, businesses, state and federal parks and forest agencies, and even city governments.

Many of the projects set out to recapture the early days of a community. The "local history" which interviewees in these popular projects recall includes legal history, business history, ethnic history, women's history, and cultural and religious history—all tied to one geographic area. Other projects have been conducted to document the history of a single institution, business, or important individual or groups, especially the ethnic minority groups. In addition, there are oral history projects which focus on a single area of regional or national concern, e.g., documenting aspects of the trade union movement in the twentieth century or a presidential administration. The result is that much oral history exists. The task for the researcher is how to find it.

Published Guides to Research Collections

Traditional bibliographic guides, although of limited help for oral history resources, are the place to begin searching for collections of papers on a desired subject. The guides may also lead to pertinent oral history sources. The first step in searching bibliographic guides is the Library of Congress *National Union Catalog of Manuscript Collections* (NUCMC). Since 1970, *NUCMC* has listed only oral history collections in transcript form and, unless an oral history is part of a larger collection of papers, those that include ten or more interviews. *NUCMC* has a thorough subject index which can be searched both by topic and personal name. A search of the main index for documentation on California history, for example, revealed entries for oral histories under "California, conservation," "California, county government," "California, wine industry," and "San Francisco waterfront," and included the names of all the interviewees in the collections. A special repository index at the end of each index volume includes a listing called "Oral History Interview Transcripts and Collections Containing Sound Recordings," The latest *NUCMC* index, 1980–1984, lists 117 collections containing oral histories/sound recordings. A survey of those 117 indicated that only a third were actual oral histories, but of that third, some were collections of ten to thirty fully transcribed interviews.

Four guides found in most research libraries will also prove useful. Every library has *Books in Print,* which lists all books in print by author, title, and subject. Under the subject *oral history,* the 1986–87 edition has 32 entries, including manuals, and lists guides such as *The Frontier Nursing Service Oral History Project: An Annotated Guide* and *The Oral History Collection of the Minnesota Historical Society.* It also listed *First Person America* by Ann Banks, a book based upon oral histories.

Research Centers Directory is an annual guide (with a biannual update) to more than nine thousand university-related and non-profit research organizations. The subject index lists twenty-two centers with oral histories, and the alphabetical index of research centers and projects reveals five beginning with the phrase *oral history.* A sample subject search under *Holocaust* revealed nine centers, of which four emphasized oral histories or, as termed in one instance, "testimonies."

The sixth edition of *Subject Collections,* compiled by Lee Ash and William G. Miller, lists seventy-eight entries under "Oral History Collections." Since these collections are not necessarily the same as those submitting information to *NUCMC,* both guides need to be checked. One collection listed only in *Subject Collections,* for example, is the New York Public Library Performing Arts Research Center collection of audio tapes, chiefly oral biographies of persons associated with dance.

The American Association for State and Local History publication, *Directory of Historical Agencies in North America,* edited by Betty Pease Smith, is an exhaustive listing of historical agencies by state and city, many of which indicate that they collect oral history. Although there is also an index to broad subject areas such as "Agriculture," this directory is most useful for finding oral history collections through geographic connections.

Published Guides to Oral Histories

For oral history *per se,* there are several dated but still useful directories and a new one about to be published. The most recent guide is the 1982 *Directory of Oral History Programs in the United States,* edited by Patsy A. Cook. The 499 programs described are listed by state and then by city. Each program description gives the principal topics and size of the collection. There is a subject index.

An older, but in some ways more useful, guide is *Oral History Collections,* edited by Alan M. Meckler and Ruth McMullin, an expansion of the 1971 Oral History Association directory, *Oral History in the United States.* The guide has brief entries to individual oral histories listed alphabetically by name and subject, followed by a section on United States oral history programs organized by state. Continuing the trial search for California topics, the authors found a listing for Governor Goodwin Knight and for *San Francisco Chronicle* editor Earl C. Behrens in the Dwight D. Eisenhower Library in Kansas, and a collection of interviews with California mining leaders, listed under "Mining Engineering," at Columbia University.

A new directory being compiled by Allen Smith at Simmons College, tentatively titled *Oral History Collections in the United States: A Directory* is being eagerly awaited by researchers. The first edition is to list some five hundred oral history programs by state and city, with an institution, subject, place name, and interviewee index. Smith and the Oral History Association expect this to be the basis of a long-term continuing directory with the prospect of online access which will make finding oral history easier in the future.

A very useful bibliography of everything published on oral history before 1984 is *Oral History: A Reference Guide and Annotated Bibliography,* compiled by Patricia Pate Havlice. By means of library search, Havlice has compiled lists of books using oral history, manuals on how to do oral history, guides to collections, articles on aspects of oral history, and bibliographies. There is an index of subjects, including, as a random sample: Alabama, Armenians, blacks, catalogs (fifty entries), Holocaust, immigrants, jazz, labor history, Richard Nixon, women, and World War II.

Specific Guides: Regional, State, Subject, Collection

There has been growing recognition by the producers of oral history collections that researchers cannot locate oral histories without more finding aids. As a result, states, regions, and organizations in various subject fields have been working to provide written and online guides to oral history sources. Bibliographies such as Havlice's, and those cited in the bibliography for this chapter, enable a researcher to locate many published oral history guides. A few are mentioned here, with a larger sampling in the bibliography.

One guide which will touch upon many research projects, the "Directory of Women's Oral History Projects and Collections," compiled by Nancy D. Mann (*Frontiers* 7, 1983), lists 48 major collections on women's history. Among the collections are, for example, Alaska Women's Oral History Collections, Anchorage Community College, 68 oral histories; Lives of Arizona Women, Arizona State University at Tempe, 200 women over 70 years of age; Civil Rights Documentation Project, Howard University, 600 interviews with civil right activists; Smith College Centennial Study, 158 alumnae of Smith College, many of them now famous; Black Women Oral History Project, Radcliffe College, 71 elderly black women leaders.

Another guide, which lists oral histories from all over the United

States because it includes collections in the Library of Congress, is James R. Heintze's *Scholars' Guide to Washington, D.C. Audio Resources: Sound Recordings in the Arts, Humanities, and Social, Physical, and Life Sciences.* The subject entry "oral history" separates oral history collections from sound recordings.

The *Annual Report and Membership Directory* of the Oral History Association regularly includes lists of oral history organizations useful to a researcher in making contacts in a specific geographic area. At present there are regional organizations for New England, the mid-Atlantic region, the Northwest, and the Southwest. States which have oral history associations are Indiana, Michigan, Minnesota, Montana, Ohio, Texas, and Wyoming. Eight states have active oral history offices or programs: Alaska, Hawaii, Idaho, Illinois, Kentucky, New Jersey, Pennsylvania, and Washington. A number of states also have a central reporting agency for oral histories. Up-to-date information can be obtained from the Oral History Association, P.O. Box 926, University Station, Lexington, Kentucky 40506. The Association's publications, *Oral History Review* and *Oral History Newsletter*, provide leads to relevant publications and collections.

Online Data Bases

The computer offers the strongest promise of facilitating the search for oral history materials. Just as with published guides and library card catalogs, information must be gathered and entered into a data base before it can be retrieved. The major national data bases, OCLC (Online Computer Library Center) and RLIN (Research Libraries Information Network), were established as a means of sharing bibliographic data for published materials. In 1983, with the introduction of the MARC AMC (Machine Readable Cataloging, Archival and Manuscripts Control) format, libraries and other agencies across the country were able to enter catalog records for unique primary source materials, including oral histories, in archives and manuscripts repositories. By mid-1987, more than 60,000 MARC AMC records had been entered into OCLC and over 100,000 into RLIN. Because of the still relatively small number of oral histories included in these numbers, online searches will provide clues to where oral histories may be found rather than lists of oral histories themselves. This situation, as is true for access to all forms of primary source materials, improves daily.

Because OCLC and RLIN are still primarily considered as internal library tools for procedures such as cataloging and interlibrary loan, there is usually no direct public access to these data bases. The researcher therefore needs to work through a librarian, often a cataloging or technical services librarian rather than a reference librarian, to effect a search. But the researcher should begin with the reference librarian to inquire whether the library is a member of OCLC or RLIN.

OCLC is oriented to title or author entry. It can be used to search for specific interviewees, but subject searches are not yet possible. Despite its limitations, OCLC should be checked because original materials cataloged in its data base will not be duplicated in RLIN.

RLIN is much more useful as a research tool because it allows for a search by subject (in Boolean combinations) as well as by author and title. Whereas in OCLC the user is able to choose whether or not to limit a search to a particular format, such as books, archival and manuscripts collections (AMC), or sound recordings, in RLIN each format is searched separately. It is important to check all formats, since some libraries may have cataloged bound oral history transcripts in book format or used the sound recordings format for oral history tapes instead of treating both as archival materials in the AMC format.

Ideally, the researcher will be able to remain with the librarian during a data base search in order to follow up leads suggested by results. Whether this is possible or not, the researcher should prepare in advance a list of (1) general subjects to be searched, (2) names of key persons who might have been interviewed, (3) any corporate names involved, such as businesses or government agencies, and (4) specific geographic areas (city, county, or state) related to the research project.

The subject phrase "oral histor#" (with "#" standing for a truncation that will retrieve both "oral history" and "oral histories") will also have to be searched in all formats. The AMC format allows for the genre entry "oral histories," which, together with an extended use of the Library of Congress subject heading "oral history" (originally intended only for works *about* oral history) by many repositories, should retrieve the bulk of useful records. With more than 22 million records in the RLIN data base, there were, at the time of this writing, over 600 entries under "oral histor#" in the books format, nearly 150 in the AMC format, but less than 10 in the sound recordings format. A trial search in the sound recordings format revealed a greater success rate if a general category of persons such as "Architects—United States" or "Women authors" were further subdivided by "interviews." This leads to the recommendation that besides a reference librarian at one's side, it is useful to have a current edition of *Library of Congress Subject Headings* close at hand.

To find lists of published directories or guides to collections, the books format search should include the following subdivisions under the general subject "oral history": directories, indexes, catalogs, guides, library resources, archival resources, and bibliographies. Once the name of an organization or agency producing relevant oral histories is identified during the search process, an additional search conducted on that corporate name might reveal additional records in any of the formats in both RLIN and OCLC. Names of interviewers and writers of introductions can also be searched. To adapt an old adage to online searching, one who already knows will find out.

Library Searches

After searching published bibliographies and online data bases, the researcher needs to consult appropriate libraries. While research libraries are the most likely repositories, there is a good chance that a town or institution library will have some oral history tapes or transcripts on its own or local history, the history of the surrounding geographic region, or related topics.

The reference librarian is again the first source of information. When inquiring about "oral histories," the researcher must bear in mind that "oral history" means only tapes to some librarians, and should specifically include "transcripts" in the request. If the researcher is told after a routine search that the library has no oral histories, that negative response should not be accepted as final, without further intensive inquiry. Like other nonbook materials, oral histories require individualized cataloging; in chronically understaffed libraries they are sometimes set aside and even forgotten. Many researchers have experienced success by gaining the cooperation of a librarian with whom they embark on a search of the library's nooks and crannies.

Other steps in an intensive inquiry should include a search of the main library catalog following the same lines recommended for online data bases. However, every library catalog is slightly different, and less formally constructed catalogs, often found in small libraries, should also be searched under subjects such as "local history." Another step is an inquiry for the names of local societies that may be collecting historical materials. The card catalog should be searched for their small publications. The groups themselves should also be contacted. Libraries often keep address cards for local organizations. Next, the researcher should ask whether the library has any special catalogs of audio-visual materials, sound recordings, or manuscripts. Finally, the researcher should ask if the library has any special collections of historical materials. These are often uncataloged or listed separately, and only an inquiry will reveal their existence.

Evaluating Oral Histories

Identifying potential oral history sources and establishing the relevancy of their subject and content are only the first steps in determining their usefulness for a particular study. The information in oral histories needs to be evaluated as carefully as that in a written text. Unlike most written documents, oral histories are the result of the complex interaction of many individuals, intentions, and purposes. A researcher should keep in mind that oral histories are recollections remembered—often many years later—and colored by succeeding events in the narrator's life. Just as the nature of memory and present knowledge must be taken into consideration, the researcher must consider the circumstances surrounding the oral history. Was it recorded as part of a project honoring the achievements of an individual, or celebrating the fiftieth anniversary of a firm, or illustrating historic injustices visited upon a minority?

The quality of the historical record created in the course of an oral history interview depends upon many factors, each of which needs to be evaluated by the researcher. The following questions illustrate areas of inquiry to be pursued in determining research value:

Is there a clear statement as to the purpose of the interview? Was it part of a larger project? How was the interview funded?

How long after the events described did the interview take place?

Is the account of events first-hand or second- or even third-hand?

How well is the narrator identified?

Is the interviewer knowledgeable in the field of the interview?

If the history is a transcript, are the principles of editing made clear? Are the questions as well as answers included?

Is the information provided consistent with other oral accounts or with documentary evidence?

Are both the tapes and the transcript available? Are there supplementary materials such as personal papers, newspaper accounts, photographs?

If part of a larger project, are interviews representing different perspectives included in the collection?

Is there evidence of careful methodology in the accompanying releases and background information?

Further directives and standards can be found in the Oral History Association's *Evaluation Guidelines* listed in this chapter's bibliography.

Responsible Use of Oral Histories

Once relevant oral histories have been located and evaluated, what are the procedures for their use? The catalog card and the introductory pages of the transcript or the data sheet of the tape should indicate any restrictions on access or use. Most oral histories are open for reading or hearing; very few require permission from the narrator or interviewer, the obtaining of which is a time-consuming procedure.

If the oral histories are open, the information they contain may be used or paraphrased. Most oral histories are also open to quotation for publication, with appropriate permission from the repository. Some oral histories, depending on the provisions of the signed release of the agreement made with the oral history organization or library, may also require the permission of the narrator and perhaps the interviewer for publication.

In some instances, a set of oral histories in a library is a duplicate of the primary set owned by another repository. For example, the Bancroft Library at the University of California at Berkeley is the West Coast repository for a set of the Black Women Oral History Project of Schlesinger Library at Radcliffe College and a set of oral histories of longtime National Park Service personnel, produced by the Harper's Ferry Center of the National Park Service. In these cases, the researcher must apply to the originating institution for permission to quote, since a copyholding repository has no authority over such oral histories beyond that of allowing the material to be used on its premises.

It is the responsibility of the researcher and the publisher to provide an adequate bibliographic citation of quoted material so that future researchers can find it easily. Although oral history citation forms have not yet been included in style manuals, the following elements are essential: names of narrator and interviewer; title of interview, if a formal title has been assigned; designation of format, such as "oral history transcript"; date and place of interview; number of pages in the transcript; name of project or series of which the oral history is a part; and name and location of repository. Based upon other citation formats, the following bibliographic entries can serve as guides for various kinds of oral histories.

Voorhis, Jerry. Tape of an interview conducted by Morton Newman and Fay Blake, 12 June 1984, for EPIC (End Poverty in California) Project. Bancroft Library, University of California, Berkeley.

Brandt, Harry. "Reminiscences of Harry Brandt," oral history interview by Joan and Robert Franklin, 1969. Transcript, 69 1.; tape recording, 1 reel. Popular Arts Project, part 2. Columbia University, Oral History Research Office, New York, N.Y.

Callister, Charles Warren. "Creating Places of Worship and Contemplation," oral history transcript, 33 pp., interviews conducted by Suzanne Riess, 1983. In *Renaissance of Religious Art and Architecture in the San Francisco Bay Area, 1946–1968*, vol. 1. Regional Oral History Office, Bancroft Library, University of California, Berkeley.

Responsible use of oral histories goes beyond verifying factual content, obtaining necessary permissions, and providing proper citations. It involves sensitive consideration of the narrators and their communities. The oral histories may deal with the personal lives of nonpublic persons who are still alive and with events that still carry an emotional impact. Oral histories differ from collections of papers; they are deliberately produced for historical purposes as the joint effort of an interviewer (usually representing a historical agency) and a narrator. The candidness of the account depends in some degree upon the confidence the narrator develops in the interviewer, and upon the reputation of the historical agency for carrying out any expectations as to how the oral history will be used. For the narrator, giving an oral history is similar to inviting a stranger into his or her home, and it is the stranger's responsibility not to take advantage of that hospitality. The user of oral histories becomes, by extension, one who enjoys guest status in the life of the narrator. For example, a study of growing up in a city over a period of three generations resulted in more than one hundred oral histories, which often gave very detailed descriptions of neighborhoods, teachers, clergy, courtship practices, prejudices, etc. The material provides a vivid picture of the eeryday life of young people over a seventy-five-year period. It could, in specific instances, cause hurt feelings and reopen old wounds if published verbatim. Researchers are allowed to use the material only with changes of names and places to assure anonymity. Responsible use not only calls for honoring such requirements, but it means recognizing when a particular use might be harmful even though there is no listed restriction.

In selecting quotations from oral histories, the decision should reflect the spirit of the narrator's account; it is not enough to quote the sentences correctly. For example, a request was made to quote certain paragraphs from the oral history of a clergyman's wife in which she had described, in lively prose, the cultured and stylish characteristics of the congregation. The request to publish those excerpts was, as stated in the release agreement, forwarded to her for approval. The ninety-year-old woman signed the approval form, but with the stipulation that the researcher also include another paragraph, in which she described the middle- and working-class segments of the congregation. To use only a part of her description would give a false impression of that church. It is the responsibility of the researcher to select and interpret the spirit as well as the letter of the oral history, and the intent of its narrator.

Conclusion

Because oral history is the liveliest of historical records for our times, it is well worth the researcher's effort to locate and incorporate it into research projects. It is not merely a supplement to the written record, which paints the background and fills in the gaps, nor is it simply a complement to more formal historical documents. By providing the personal, inside view of events, and by revealing human motivations, emotional responses, and subjective evaluations left unrecorded in print in this day of telephones, electronic mail, and shredding machines, oral history can provide information about the past that exists in no other form.

ROMAN DRAZNIOWSKY

11. CARTOGRAPHIC SOURCES

Human beings have collected information about their activities and surroundings throughout the centuries. One of the methods used to preserve information for future generations has been its presentation in graphic form. As a result, cartographic materials in various sizes and formats have been a part of archives, libraries, and historical collections for a very long time. Cartographic materials appear as single or multiple sheets in bound or loose-leaf sets, as supportive material in other works, and as self-sufficient documents. Maps have been prepared on such different materials as clay, papyrus, stone, silver, gold, vellum, silk, paper, and plastic. Because of their diversity and manner of presenting information, maps provide a unique, as well as sometimes misunderstood, source.

The Nature of Maps

What is a map? The question sounds superfluous. After all, almost everyone uses maps, and everyone recognizes a map. As is the case with many other seemingly simple phenomena, a definition is difficult. Two basic sources define a map as:

a conventional representation, normally to scale and usually on a flat medium, of a selection of material or abstract features on or in relation to the surface of the Earth or of a heavenly body.[1]

a graphic representation, usually on a plane surface and at an established scale, of natural and manmade features on or under the surface of the earth or other planetary body. The features are positioned as accurately as possible, usually relative to a coordinate reference system. Also, a graphic representation of a part of the whole of the celestial sphere.[2]

K. A. Zalishchev argued that

> maps find their use in all spheres of scientific, economic and cultural activities. They are indispensable for a detailed regis- tration, analysis and objective evaluation of natural conditions and resources of labor and productive forces, as well as of the multiform services system (education, public health, trade, etc.). . . They are used to rule a state and to control its economy, they serve for the purpose of planning, rational distribution of productive forces, which ensures the saving of material, labor and financial means. . . . . Maps show natural conditions, population and political systems of individual countries and of the world as a whole, thus serving the purpose of mutual acquaintance and, hence, mutual understanding between nations.[3]

Map Elements and Map Use

A major value of a map to the researcher is that it provides information quickly, utilizing a relatively limited amount of space. No other medium can intelligently present the spatial distribution of phenomena. Frustrations and disappointments will be avoided if researchers realize that a map is a representation of reality in a reduced and simplified form, and, as such, has limitations. Map symbolism, use of colors, scale, and projections may contribute to misunderstanding. Despite their great research value, maps are created by humans and therefore not always completely objective and free of inaccuracies.

To use maps successfully the researcher must have a basic knowl- edge of map elements, including map terminology. Although no one would expect to make intelligent use of a book written in a language with which he is not familiar, many researchers expect to be able to use a map without any difficulty. To achieve optimal results, the researcher must identify and retrieve the map best suited to the research project. In locating the proper map, the researcher must consider area, topic (subject), time period, scale, and projection. Each of these will be discussed individually.

Area

Delineation of the area to be studied is the first step in locating the desired map. Although seemingly an easy task, the researcher may find difficulties related to geographical location and size of the area; toponymic, or place name, problems may occur. The size of the area and the amount of topical detail required will determine the necessary map scale and projection. Large-scale maps provide a great deal of information on topography, man-made features, and toponymy, but they cover a relatively small area. To cover a larger area at a large scale, more than one sheet must be used. An increase in the number of sheets may inconvenience the researcher who is an infrequent map user. A single-sheet map which provides uninterrupted coverage of a large area is limited in the amount of detailed information it contains. This type of map provides general information, geographically locating an area in relation to the surrounding regions.

The best method of determining the geographical location of a given area on a map is by means of geographical coordinates, which are indicated on most maps by north-south lines known as *longitudes* or *meridians,* and east-west lines known as *latitudes* or *parallels.* This system of lines, superimposed on maps or globes, is known as the geographical grid. The spacing between parallels and meridians is expressed in terms of degrees, minutes, and seconds. By indicating degrees, minutes, and seconds of latitude and longitude, any place on earth can be easily located. Geographical gazetteers locate places by citing degrees of latitude and longitude. For example, to locate Chicago on a map, it is necessary to ascertain the geographical coordinates, which are 41° 53′ north latitude and 87° 37′ west longitude, based on the Greenwich prime (0°) meridian longitude.

Researchers should note that, for a long time, the Greenwich meridian was not recognized internationally as the prime (0°)

meridian. As a result, maps were based on various prime meridians, including Ferro, Paris, Pulkovo, Washington, D.C., Philadelphia, and others. To locate a place on a map based on the Washington, D.C. meridian when using degrees based on the Greenwich meridian, the researcher must remember the difference in degrees of longitude between the two prime meridians. Not being aware of the prime meridian used on a map can have disastrous consequences. Using the Washington, D.C., meridian (longitude), Washington, D.C., is located at 0°, but according to the Greenwich meridian, it is at 77° west longitude. Similarly, Chicago is located at 10° 35' west longitude using the Washington, D.C., meridian, but it is at 87° 37' west longitude using the Greenwich meridian. The difference between the Washington and Greenwich prime meridians is 77° 02'. Since Chicago is located 10° 35' west of Washington, D.C., it is necessary to add 10° 35' to 77° 02', the number of degrees between Washington and Greenwich, and on maps based on Greenwich prime meridian, Chicago will be at 87° 37' west longitude. Using degree values based on Washington prime meridian to locate Chicago on a map based on Greenwich prime meridian, Chicago would be located in the Atlantic Ocean, some 120 miles off the coast of Portugal. Such a mistake is unlikely today when all maps are based on the Greenwich meridian, but old maps must be used with caution. Although the geographical grid system may initially seem complicated, it provides pinpoint accuracy even when no place name appears on the map.

However, on some road maps and maps in older atlases, locating a required area is possible only when the name appears on the map. At such times the researcher must use a combination of letters and numbers which refer to a grid system of squares printed on the map. The desired place is located within the appropriate square.

Another problem related to locating an area or city on a map is name change. Cities are most frequently involved, although the problem can occur with countries. For example, St. Petersburg, Petrograd, and Leningrad are all names given to the same city at different times. Because of these name changes a researcher could have difficulty locating that city on maps from different time periods. The African country known as Upper Volta recently became Burkina Faso; because of political changes, the name of the region known as eastern Europe is being replaced on maps by central Europe. To avoid misunderestandings, it is advisable to use city, country, and other place names exactly as the local population does. English-speaking people for many years spelled and pronounced foreign place names incorrectly: Warsaw instead of *Warszawa*, Prague for *Praha*, Moscow for *Moskva*, Florence for *Firenze*, Venice for *Venezia*, etc. *Russia* is still used as a synonym for the Union of Soviet Socialist Republics, although the name actually refers to one of the fifteen republics within the USSR.

Topic

Every map is prepared for a specific purpose. Although in most cases more than one topic is represented on a map, the dominant topic determines where the map will be placed within a given classification system. For example, a map which indicates individual countries and their administrative units by very distinct boundary lines or different colors may also provide information on roads, railroads, and place names, and even indicate a general outline of relief, showing topography. Nevertheless, because of the detailed portrayal of political divisions, the map will be classified as a political map.

Because map classification does not provide complete bibliographical data, a researcher must consult the catalog of the collection for that information. Classification brings maps with similar characteristics together in major topical divisions, such as physical, economic, or political. By approaching a map collection through major classification divisions, the researcher will find it much easier to locate a desired map.

Time Period

The next important element in locating the proper map is a time frame. The researcher should realize that usually there are two dates involved: the date which relates to the information represented on the map, and the date of publication. These dates are not always the same.

When reference is made to boundary changes which occurred

after World War II, the publication date of a map is not of prime concern, as long as the changes are represented. However, in planning a trip or locating a new settlement, the most up-to-date information is required, and the publication date becomes important. Outdated maps can lead to unpleasant and costly mistakes. Unfortunately, some map publishers do not date their maps, for commercial reasons. When using an undated map, the researcher can establish an approximate date by checking features which indicate the age of the maps in question. Features such as name changes, new roads, boundary changes, or water reservoirs, which can be linked to a specific date, will provide an approximate date of publication.

Scale

Obviously, the world cannot be represented on a map at full size. To represent and comprehend the spatial distribution of phenomena, the world, or any part of it, must be "scaled down," i.e., reduced to a specific scale. Map scale is the ratio of the distance between two points on a map and the distance between the same two points in actuality. That simple principle represents a very complex concept involving the transformation of the real world into a reduced version on a map.

On a map, scale can be indicated in three different ways: through the use of descriptive words, such as "inches to miles" or "miles to inches"; by a representative fraction, such as "1:24,000"; or by a graphic scale. The descriptive method has been used mostly by the British. Representative fraction and graphic scales are accepted universally.

In understanding the use of scale, the researcher must be aware that map projections can contribute to scale distortion. As a result, map scale generally does not remain constant over all parts of a map. It is important for the researcher to know that scale regulates the amount of information presented on a map. Maps at scales of 1:24,000 or larger cover relatively small areas, but they provide much more information about physical or man-made features than maps of 1:1,000,000 scale or smaller. Small-scale maps cover a much larger area but provide less information on the features of the mapped region.

Projection

To portray the earth's three-dimensional form on a two-dimensional map without distortion is an impossible task. For centuries, cartographers have tried to find a satisfactory solution to this problem. By developing a variety of map projections based upon "any systematic arrangement of meridians and parallels, portraying the curved surface of the sphere, or spheroid upon a plane,"[4] the problem has been partially solved. Every projection is designed to preserve one of the following properties: shape of the depicted area, size of the depicted area, or the correct relationship of the distance between two points on the map and the same two points on the earth. Since no one projection is capable of preserving all of these properties, a certain amount of distortion must be accepted. Nevertheless, by choosing a map projection to fit specific needs, it is possible, by means of mathematical control, to distribute the amount of distortion and to maintain accuracy in some areas at the expense of others. Map users should be aware of the properties and distortions inherent in different map projections in order to select the proper map for their needs.

Use of Cartographic Material

As depositories of information related to specific regions, archives and regional history collections can be gold mines for researchers. Although the holdings of individual collections vary, basic regional cartographic materials are almost always available. Self-sustaining single maps and county atlases, also known as plat books, predominate in collections of this type. However, maps included as supportive material in historical records or other publications must not be overlooked by the researcher. Cartographic materials accompanying manuscripts deserve special attention because of the original information they provide.

To utilize cartographic materials fully, the researcher should have access to reference materials which include gazetteers, map indexes, almanacs, and basic publications on cartography. The cartographic holdings of regional historical societies often consist largely of state- and federal-government publications, since they are relatively inexpensive. Since the discarding or weeding policy of these institutions is frequently more conservative than that of academic or public libraries, it is sometimes possible to locate unique early editions of large-scale maps, including United States Geological Survey topographic quadrangles. This out-of-print material has been discarded in many instances from map collections as newer editions were published. Old topographic maps provide a wealth of information on physical changes and document man's impact on the environment when compared with more recent maps of the same area.

The publishers of county atlases almost certainly did not realize how important these works would become as sources of information for future researchers. Clara LeGear of the Library of Congress wrote that American county atlases "have no counterpart in other countries, where cadastral surveys are issued by governmental organizations rather than by commerical publishers. That these atlases have satisfied a cultural need is apparent from their great popularity and . . . wide distribution. . . . [They] now have considerable historical significance."[5]

County atlases provide not only cadastral maps with the names of property owners, but also biographies of local residents, pictures of their farms, agricultural statistics, and all sort of advertisements. The numerous editions of county atlases, and the wealth of information they contain, offer researchers of all kinds—historians, geographers, surveyors, genealogists, realtors, and even tax officials—the opportunity to utilize them to reconstruct the social and physical environments of the past. County atlases are indispensable sources for researchers.

One of the important properties of maps is their ability to show regional distribution of phenomena in graphic form. As a result, maps are used to enhance the written text in books and periodicals. They comprise an integral part of the publication and function as support material; divorcing them from the text disrupts the unity of the document. The separated parts have less value in research.

Although maps in books, periodicals, and other publications

provide very useful information, their retrieval can be difficult.[6] Because of inadequate indexing and a complete lack of cataloging, the maps that are not easily accessible remain lost for practical purposes. The situation with manuscript maps is similar. Just as a manuscript text reflects original work, a manuscript map reflects an original survey. Its research value is unique, providing the presenting researcher with the view of its creator free of the influence of other surveyors.

In any cartographic collection, the most important reference tool is the catalog of its holdings. The catalog provides bibliographical data on publications and indicates their location within the collection. Before retrieving and/or handling cartographic materials, the researcher can save time and avoid frustration by checking on rules and methods with the staff member in charge.

Next to the catalog, the most important reference sources for researchers are cartobibliographies and gazetteers. A cartobibliography is an index of cartographic materials usually arranged by form: single-sheet maps, maps in publications, atlases, and globes. It may also offer chronological access to regional topical coverage. Because cartobibliographies do not always provide separate entries for relatively small geographical areas, it is advisable to search entries for larger regions which might include coverage of the desired area. A gazetteer is a dictionary of geographical place names. Geographical dictionaries and gazetteers are indispensable for finding the location of physical and man-made features, names of regions, cities, and other settlements, as well as for tracing name changes.

It is impossible in a brief chapter to identify all of the problems which a researcher might encounter in locating cartographic materials. Successful research depends upon a knowledge of the nature of maps and the ability to locate and utilize appropriate material with guidance from a map librarian.

OTTILIA KOEL

12. HISTORICAL SITE DOCUMENTATION —A CASE STUDY

Using the Soldiers' and Sailors' Monument in New Haven, Connecticut, as an example, this chapter illustrates how much overlap exists in documentary materials on a historic site, how different kinds of records and papers can be used to document the same hypothesis, and how much of the outcome of the research depends upon the skill, purpose, and imagination of the researcher.

In 1987, New Haven celebrated the one hundredth anniversary of the dedication of the Soldiers' and Sailors' Monument, located on the summit of East Rock Park. The erection of this monument was the culmination of efforts toward developing one of the earliest and most beautiful parks of the city. Several groups have conducted research to document this historic site, establishing facts and recollecting the legends that often surround such sites.

Turning first to a history of New Haven parks by Vincent M. Reynolds, we find that in 1877 Noah Porter, the president of Yale College, attended a meeting of "The Club," a social and literary group in New Haven, where he urged the members to establish a park on East Rock. Members of The Club got busy and obtained land and funds for the project. Gifts were made in the understanding that the proposed park would be managed by a commission made up in part by citizens who were not members of the city government, to secure a nonpartisan and disinterested management. After the common council accepted the offer, East Rock Park was chartered by the Connecticut General Assembly in 1880, and the first commission was formed with Simeon E. Baldwin, W. W. Farnam, and C. C. Blatchley as its citizen members.

However, another history of New Haven, by Rollin G. Osterweis, reports that in the fall of 1876 a special committee, headed by Mayor Henry Lewis and Alderman Simeon E. Baldwin, was appointed to consider the question of purchasing a new public park. Yale president Noah Porter, who was a nature lover and hiker, persuaded the committee to convert the East Rock area into a park, and East Rock Park was chartered in 1880 by action of the state legislature, with 144 acres of land in New Haven and 209 in the adjoining city of Hamden. Of the 353 acres, 87 were given by various donors and the rest purchased after condemnation proceedings; the principal donors were John W. Bishop and Yale College. A board of commissioners of East Rock Park was charged with development of the project.

The East Rock Park Commission of 1880 evolved by 1899 into the New Haven Park Commission, which in 1900 became the Park Department of the City of New Haven. (Since 1975, its title has been the Department of Parks, Recreation and Trees.) When the New Haven Commission on Public Parks was created in 1889, three members of the East Rock Park Commission, Simeon E. Baldwin, Henry T. Blake, and Henry F. English, secretary, were carried over to the new commission. Henry English became the first secretary and treasurer of the new commission and maintained that office for 58 years. The new park commission issued its first report in 1890. The minutes of the meetings of the East Rock Park Commission (1880–89) are in the Whitney Library of the New Haven Colony Historical Society; all subsequent records are in the Department of Parks, Recreation and Trees (1900 to date).

Work on the park was well underway in 1884, and the commissioners had even come to terms with the eccentric Milton J. Stewart, the owner of the top of the rock who had built a forty-foot boat next to his house there, ready for the eventuality of another Flood. Successive developments included the completion of Farnam Drive in 1882–83 (gift of Henry Farnam), English Drive in 1885–86 (gift of James English), Trowbridge Drive in 1896–97, the Farm in 1920, Hillhouse Drive and the Pardee Rose Garden, both in 1935, and Mitchell Drive in 1939–40. These and other additions were all realized through donations, many of which commemorate the donors: Bishop Gate was erected in 1896 in memory of the first donor, John W. Bishop; Blake Field honors Henry T. Blake, the first president of the New Haven Park Commission.

A look at the early minutes gives no date for Session 1; Session

2 is dated April 28, 1880, and Session 54, July 17, 1889. The first entries document subscriptions to the park fund in terms of land and money, and provide a roster of the commissioners: Mayor Bigelow, Alderman Stoddard, Councilman Woolsey from the city, and S. E. Baldwin, W. W. Farnam, and C. C. Blatchley as citizen members. At the end of the first year, the minutes report that much of the time had been taken up with determining the layout of the park and hearing from numerous interested parties, with the Board of Road Commissioners accepting or amending the proposals.

In March 1882, the commissioners voted to have the mayor and W. W. Farnam obtain from Donald G. Mitchell "his price for making a survey and plan for developing the park." In September Mitchell's report was read and accepted, and "the accompanying map was directed to be suspended in the Mayor's Office and the Mayor was authorized to place it on exhibition in the window of some suitable store on Chapel Street." (The map now hangs in the office of the Deputy Director of the Department of Parks, Recreation and Trees.) In February 1883, payment of $75 was authorized for printing Mitchell's report. The payment was an outside contribution, rather than taken from the budget of the East Rock Park Commission. Mitchell, a man of letters who had already donated his landscaping talents to the east side of town when he proposed a plan for the "harmonious development" of the new park to the Commission. "The bold picturesqueness of the site does not invite the niceties of conventional gardening," wrote Mitchell, and accordingly he planned roads leading to the highest point in the park leaving the woods untouched. He proposed a lookout tower on the summit, but in 1884 it was decided under pressure from citizens' and veterans' groups that a monument be erected on the summit "to commemorate the New Haven men who had died in the Revolution, the War of 1812, the Mexican War, and the War for the Union."

Constantly cognizant that a public park was to be enjoyed by a large number of citizens, the commissioners created and amended bylaws, such as "no person shall ride or drive on any road within the Park at a faster gait than seven miles per hour," and "no threatening, abusive, boisterous, insulting or indecent language, gesture or conduct shall be used or had on said Park." Other prohibitions included the exclusion of animals other than dogs; injuring or marking in any way the trees, shrubs, plants, etc.; carrying firearms; appearing naked; making fire; injuring birds; discharging firecrackers; quarrying stone (they had considerable trouble with this item); abandoning bottles, paper, or other rubbish. Ironically, we read in today's local New Haven press that although East Rock is one of the city's largest and most beautiful parks, it has fallen victim, after decades of neglect, to serious vandalism, crime, litter, and maintenance problems.

In 1884 a restaurant was approved for the park. (In 1986 it was suggested again that a food concession be opened at the summit to establish a constant presence because of the belief that "people behave better when they are being watched.") The 1884 proposal was to encourage citizens to spend more time in the park. That of 1986 was to discourage an undesirable element from using the park. In 1884 a superintendent was hired whose pay "while in charge of a force of laborers [was] to be $2.75 for each working day, and half that amount when prevented by bad weather from working, and while not in charge of laborers to be $1.75 per day." In 1885 a Mr. Elby asked permission to start a museum on the summit and was denied permission a year later. Meanwhile, an Eli Whitney was given permission on several occasions to take "a few loads of sand from the Park" and stone, also, "if he has the right to do so."

The Soldiers' and Sailors' Monument ws first mentioned in the minutes of 1884 when a liaison committee of Messrs. Baldwin, Whitney, and Blatchley was appointed to cooperate with the Town Committee. Consequently, Messrs. Farnam and Baldwin were appointed as a conference committee to confer with Mr. Mitchell concerning the cost of a detailed layout of the top of the park.

Local records are often scattered. For instance, the Mitchell maps that relate to East Rock Park are divided among the map collections of the Sterling Memorial Library of Yale University, the New Haven Department of Parks, Recreation and Trees, and the Whitney Library of the New Haven Colony Historical Society. The Whitney Library also has a collection of Mitchell papers (1881–92). In addition to the "Suggestions for Monument of Summit of East Rock Park" executed in 1887, the papers contain the manuscript supplement to Mitchell's 1882 report to the commission in which he writes lovingly of the surrounding nature, the largest charm of which "must always lie in the commanding view—its savagery of cliffs, and unkempt and wild tufts of foliage." Mitchell gives detailed suggestions for the development of the summit as the monument site, treating the grading, lawn, carriage stand, trees, music stand, fountains, restaurant, paths, seats, and flower and shrub plantings, and referring to the accompanying map. He concludes by insisting that the ground features of the park must always be dominant because "flowers or garish niceties must be dealt with coyly; perhaps not dealt with at all." He appends a list of proposed plants, shrubs, trees, etc.

Donald Grant Mitchell (1822–1908) was a grandson of Stephen Mix Mitchell, member of the Continental Congress and Chief Justice of Connecticut. After graduation from Yale in 1841, and in order to counteract a family tendency toward tuberculosis, he lived on an ancestral farm where he wrote about rural things. When an appointment as clerk to the United States consul in Liverpool, England, ended because of ill health, Mitchell traveled throughout the Isle of Jersey, the British Isles, and the Continent, often walking to build his strength. In the years between 1846 and 1855, he lived in Washington and New York writing for newspapers and unenthusiastically reading law. During this period he began signing his output "Ik Marvel." In 1848 he covered the revolution in Paris; several of his books appeared soon thereafter, e.g., *Reveries of a Bachelor*. In 1853 Mitchell married, and after a short term as consul in Venice, he bought "Edgewood," a farm in Westville (New Haven), which became a model for farming, home building, and town planning. While living at Edgewood, he aided the New Haven Board of Park Commissioners in designing and developing city parks, especially East Rock Park. He wrote several books about Edgewood, and his collected works, published in 1907, were called the Edgewood Edition. The Donald G. Mitchell Memorial Library is one of many tributes to him in Westville.

Another manuscript collection in the Whitney Library, probably the most important one for the documentation of the monument, is the Records (1881–94) of the Soldiers' and Sailors' Monument Committee. The Records include the complete archives of the committee and consist of the minutes of meetings and other business, correspondence, architectural drawings, blueprints and renderings, financial statements, and scrapbooks of clippings from presses, both local and long-distance. Apparently as far back as 1879, the Admiral Foote Post of the Grand Army of the Republic had petitioned the city for a memorial to honor their commander and the soldiers who fell. In 1881, various committees commenced work toward the realization of the monument, and an extensive correspondence with architects, marble and stone suppliers, etc., began. The idea of attaching bronze tablets listing the names of the soldiers and sailors being commemorated was first proposed in 1885, but installation was not completed until 1894, well after the 1887 dedication of the monument; the delay was caused in part by the difficulty in collecting the names, rank, and place of death of the veterans. The cornerstone was laid in 1886 and the monument dedicated on June 17, 1887, and both events were attended by thousands of people. The day of dedication is often referred to as the greatest celebration in New Haven's history. Local papers carried special "Monument Day" supplements elaborating on the happenings of the day, with photographs of the huge parade and distinguished guests and speakers. Even *Frank Leslie's Illustrated News* on June 18, 1887, the day following the dedication of the memorial, carried an illustration of the artist's conception of the Soldiers' and Sailors' Monument.

In documenting a historical site (or any research project), the need, imagination, determination, and skill of the researcher determines the use of a variety of sources. For an anniversary of a historic site, usually there is reliance on published materials, often newspaper articles, which can be scanned on microfilm or in scrapbooks compiled by interested historians, participants, members of committees, and the like. Research for legal purposes or scholarly pursuits involves the use of original source materials which include both private papers and public documents. In this study, for instance, the annual publications of the City of New Haven and the Park Commission summarize the actions taken by these agencies during the report year, but much more can be learned from the verbatim records of the meetings which led to the decisions being made. Original minutes of meetings are preferable to the printed annual reports. Much information can be gathered also from recollections or diaries of committee members or others who were instrumental in carrying out various actions. Depending on the focus of the research, much can often be gleaned from seemingly irrelevant papers; for instance, to document the development of the landscaping of East Rock Park, one could use other collections in the Whitney Library, such as the records of the New Haven Chamber of Commerce, which was involved in many aspects of the park development; the records of the Garden Club of New Haven, which has had a special interest in the beautification of the city and its parks; and even the papers of Mary Laetitia Verdery Pierson who, during 1954–55, made plans for the reconstruction of the Pardee Rose Garden in East Rock Park, the original plans and drawings for which are in the collection. Maps, as previously mentioned, are scattered in at least three different places, as are the deeds of land transfers (Connecticut State Library, Hall of Records of New Haven, private papers of families and individuals). Newspapers, which are useful for providing dates and names, are not always reliable; this is generally true of city directories as well. Architectural drawings are sometimes retained by the architect, but others are kept by the agency which commissioned the work; architectural drawings, especially the better ones, typically become fugitives which may turn up anywhere and anytime. For example, the Whitney Library recently acquired a large cache of architectural drawings by a prominent local architect whose summer home in Maine had housed the rolled drawings for over sixty years.

Although the course of public documents is mandated, many disappear intentionally or inadvertently. The course of private papers ranges, at best, from the oblivion of family retention to, at worst, the not infrequent, willful destruction of business records or family papers. On the local history level there is often more pride and solicitude in preserving genealogies than the records of a family business or the papers of a gifted family member. The concept of local history does not seem to include the preservation of records.

The bibliography to this chapter illustrates the types of materials that can be used for the documentation of historic sites. Materials for this report have been found in the Hall of Records of New Haven; the New Haven Department of Parks, Recreation and Trees; the Whitney Library of the New Haven Colony Historical Society; and in Sterling Memorial Library of Yale University.

OTTILIA KOEL

13. Genealogical Research

If genealogy is an auxiliary discipline of history, genealogists are historians whose concern is the history of their own family or of other families. Why is there then a conflict between genealogists and librarians and archivists? Old myths die hard or not at all. The one about genealogists as little old ladies in sneakers, trying to prove that they are "holier than thou," asking endless questions but unwilling or unable to acquire appropriate research skills, seems to have lingered for a long time. In the April 1969 issue of the *Yale University Library Gazette* we read that "the Yale Library used to frown on genealogical books because they attracted genealogical 'cranks' to the Library. Let these eager old ladies go to the Genealogy Room at the New York Public Library—we didn't want them."

It is possible that some of the American aversion toward genealogy comes from times when genealogical research was undertaken to prove purity of descent, to flatter the vanity of aristocratic families, or to satisfy the tribal need for continuity of the clan—the birthright to property and power. During medieval times genealogical research in similar vein was undertaken because of inheritance laws and the desire to maintain the privileges attained by a hereditary upper class. Because of this, family histories were often tainted with inaccuracy, and genealogy was equated with pedigree mongering. Such histories, invariably treating leading families and their prominent and/or notorious members, became a standard research source for biographers, geographers, and historians, albeit one which presented a historical account viewed from the top down.

An upsurge of social studies seems to have reversed this trend. With the growing interest in urban development, the labor movement, ethnic and minority life, our cultural heritage, and genetic studies, local histories are now frequently written from the viewpoint of the anonymous families, i.e., from the bottom up.

Privilege by birth is not compatible with the democratic ideals of Americans, and therefore may have little appeal for them. But patriotism is another matter. Long before the popularity of quantitative social studies and histories, many Americans were involved in the pursuit of family history out of patriotic pride. The great number of patriotic and hereditary societies that were established during the last century require strict genealogical proof of eligibility for membership; under this banner genealogy became a respectable vocation and avocation for Americans whether their ancestors came from Africa or arrived on the *Mayflower*.

At the same time, changes also came about among librarians and archivists. Although these groups consider themselves as belonging to two different professions, as in many ways they do, they have one very important thing in common: they both exist for the purpose of organizing and storing information to make it easily retrievable and accessible to everyone. The problem of teaching researchers to communicate with the card catalog no longer exists in many libraries where resources are now accessible by computer and pooled in networks of libraries and archival repositories. The writer of the previously mentioned 1969 article, for instance, would not have to send anyone from Yale to the New York Public Library, because both institutions now belong to the Research Libraries Group, which has pooled resources; the "genealogical crank" can now request that materials be sent from New York to New Haven.

Although cooperation among libraries makes materials more accessible by spreading the burden of service between large and small research collections, the cost of converting to automated systems and acquiring the necessary hardware has been, and remains, a costly proposition for many libraries. Librarians and archivists often justify the high expense to administrators by citing the large number of researchers served. An impressive percentage of that number is composed of researchers in history and its auxiliary disciplines, genealogy among them. Librarians and archivists have become familiar with the needs of genealogists and the large variety of ways in which scholarly genealogical research is being done in intellectual pursuit of history and the other social sciences in their varied ramifications.

Since much of the information needed to support genealogical research is found in original sources, genealogists are diligent patrons of archival repositories, from the impressive National Archives and Records Administration (NARA), where they make up more than 50 percent of all users, to small business archives in public libraries and historical societies. If librarians and archivists complain that genealogists often lack basic research skills, genealogists complain that archival collections are not arranged with the user in mind. Although some collections are well indexed and their computers user-friendly, it is hard to locate information on small geographic entities, individuals with changed names, or families whose names have undergone a change in spelling. When working with collections of municipal records, genealogists find little professional help.

Genealogical researchers need experience, an analytic mind, critical judgment, and special skills such as the ability to read Colonial handwriting and understand the Colonial calendar, but most of all they need meticulous methodology. Experienced genealogists warn beginners against relying on printed genealogies, undocumented sources, lack of proof, and jumping to conclusions; they recommend care and attention to detail. Donald L. Jacobus, for instance, considers printed genealogies good only "to aid the uninformed lovers of genealogy."

Courses in basic genealogical research are given by many archives, libraries, and genealogical societies on the national, state, and local level. There are also numerous how-to books on the market which teach basic skills and identify resources. Although the quality varies, most can assist the budding genealogist; all have at least one chapter on finding aids. In the abundance of reference works there are indexes to monographic family histories and to articles in local history and genealogical periodicals, gazetteers, geographical dictionaries and city directories, heraldic and family-name histories; there are also indexes to census records, passenger-arrival lists, published vital statistics, church and cemetery archives, inventories, and catalogs of the holdings of such large collections as the Library of Congress and the Newberry Library.

There is no end to the list of original source materials that can be useful to genealogists: federal census records, pension and military records, passenger lists, citizenship papers, tax- and voter-registration lists, probate and land records, county court records, vital statistics records, church registers, legal and financial transactions, insurance and real estate maps and atlases, school records, business archives, membership lists, and so on. A resourceful researcher is able to find information in the most unexpected place; for example, a patron of the Whitney Library of the New Haven Colony Historical Society was pleased to discover missing data in the personnel records of the business archives of an old New Haven hotel which no longer exists. Many federal records housed in the National Archives and Records Administration which are useful to genealogists are also available on microfilm at NARA or its eleven regional archives centers. The microfilm version can be purchased or borrowed for a fee. The steady increase in records being made available by either the record–generating agency or a commercial firm greatly enhances research possibilities for genealogists.

State records can usually be found in the state archives; local court records, in the court libraries/archives; county, town, and other local records, in municipal archives, state archives, courthouses, town clerks' offices, etc. Family histories in manuscript form usually represent a compiler's work that relies on correspondence with members and friends of the family, on use of family records including photographs and Bible entries, and on biographical information and obituaries culled from newspapers. Researchers are advised to use these with as much caution as printed family histories.

Many libraries can support genealogical research. Some are devoted entirely to it; other general research libraries have collected excellent holdings. A few of the outstanding ones are the Library of Congress, the New York Public Library, the Newberry Library in Chicago, and the New England Historic and Genealogical Society in Boston.

Special mention has to be made of the important cooperation genealogists have received of late from the library of the Genealogical Society of the Church of Jesus Christ of Latter-Day Saints in Salt Lake City. The Mormons are dedicated to researching their ancestors out of a sense of religious duty and have created a major, if not *the* major, repository of information for the genealogist. They have scanned a large part of the world for records, many of which they have microfilmed. The microfilm negatives are deposited in a famous granite vault outside of Salt Lake City, but positive copies and other resources are shared with seekers of information, mainly through the branch libraries of the Church which (at this writing) number 700. The time, funds, and expertise the Mormons have put into this endeavor are impressive. In their use of technology, they are well ahead of other research collections, having created a gigantic data base and an index with over one million name entries. They have microfilmed public records, church and cemetery records, vital records, family histories, and other relevant source materials. For many years the Mormons have been of great service to genealogical researchers, and it is hoped that this mutually beneficial cooperation will continue to grow.

The increasing demand for genealogical materials has created a need for more reference manuals and handbooks and for reprinting family and local histories, which were typically produced in limited editions. Because some reprint publishers are less reputable than others, caution is advised when materials are purchased in case they have been reprinted under new titles without mention of this fact. The *Gale Genealogy and Local History Series* of the Gale Research Company is a treasure trove of information for genealogists, beginning and experienced. Several other companies are currently searching for and reprinting out-of-print items.

It is recommended that researchers acquaint themselves with the rules and regulations of the collection in which they intend to search. Rules in research institutions are not designed as a personal affront to the researcher, but to preserve collections containing unique and perishable items. Ample time should be allowed for genealogical research, so important sources and references are not missed. Researchers should explain to the archivists and librarians what they want and should not hesitate to ask questions. The archivists and librarians are there to help, but researchers should not expect them to do the research for them. It should be noted that most libraries with genealogical holdings maintain a list of genealogists who can be hired to undertake searches for individual clients.

BONNIE JO CULLISON

14. THE PRESERVATION
OF ARCHIVAL MATERIAL

A significant portion of the cumulative knowledge of mankind exists on paper-based records. Few are aware that a major share of these records is in an advanced state of deterioration. Some research institutions estimate that tens of thousands of books in their collections will suffer damage if they are used just one more time. A recent assessment of the holdings at the National Archives estimates that about a half billion pages of historical information are at a high risk of being permanently lost.[1]

Up to the present the initiative to save the vast holdings of libraries, archives, and historical societies has come from the library-archive community. Mary Linn Ritzenthaler has pointed out that "collection materials clearly need an advocate, and no one is better suited to the job than the archivist or curator."[2] However, as an understanding of the extent and significance of the problem grows, the sphere of advocacy grows apace. Systematic efforts are being undertaken to insure that limited resources return maximum gains. Scholars and researchers are becoming involved in establishing guiding principles to foster cooperative preservation activities among many institutions. Scholars' knowledge of the literature of their fields permits critical evaluations for determining resource priorities and allocations.

On a more mundane level, scholars, as users, have a direct impact on the survival of research materials. Paper-based records are vulnerable, and the causes of their deterioration are complex and interrelated. To understand the journey from creation to crumbling, it is important to know about the nature of paper and the multitude of factors that contribute to its demise. Armed with this knowledge, researchers will be better equipped to play a role as preservation advocates.

It is a fact of nature that organic matter and objects made from organic materials begin to deteriorate as soon as they are formed. Paper, since its invention in China in the second century, has most commonly been fabricated from plant fibers. Cellulose, which gives plant cells most of their strength, is the basic ingredient in paper. Cellulose is built from glucose molecules which form long chainlike structures. These cellulose chains bond together chemically and physically to form fibers. Paper is made by beating the cellulose fibers and mixing them with water to form a slurry, which is deposited on a screen. After the water drains through the screen, the fibrous sheet that remains is transferred to a flat surface and pressed. During pressing, a chemical and physical bond is formed between the intricately entwined cellulose fibers, giving paper its strength. As these bonds break down over time, the paper is weakened.

The rate at which the breakdown of paper occurs is influenced by several factors: the environment in which it is housed and used, including the temperature, humidity, light, and air quality; the manner in which it is stored and handled; and its own chemical composition.

Of these factors, chemical composition can be the most insidious. Most paper, especially paper manufactured since the midnineteenth century, contains the seeds of its own destruction, or "inherent vice," as it is known in the insurance world. Papermaking was introduced to Europe by the Moors in Spain, at about 1085. For the first several centuries that paper was made, it was produced by hand and was relatively "pure," with few deleterious additives to the basic recipe of plant fibers (usually cotton or linen rags), water, and a sizing agent such as gelatin. (Sizing paper produces a smooth surface suitable for writing; ink feathers on the surface of unsized paper.) The methods of beating the plant fibers resulted in long, strong cellulose fibers. Paper made in this way was, and generally remains, strong and flexible.

However, as demand for paper increased, various stages of production were accelerated by using chemicals such as alum, resin, and chlorine. Unfortunately, these chemicals gradually degrade to form acids which cause a chemical breakdown (acid hydrolysis) of the bonds between the glucose units of the cellulose chain. As the cellulose chains break into increasingly shorter lengths, the physical bonding between fibers is weakened and the paper becomes brittle. New methods were introduced to accelerate the maceration of fibers prior to sheet formation. These resulted in shorter fibers and a weaker paper.

Life expectancy of paper reached an all-time low in the mid-nineteenth century, with the introduction of groundwood pulp paper. As the demand for more and cheaper paper exceeded the supply of rags available, wood became the primary source of cellulose fiber for paper production. Initially, the wood was ground mechanically with little attempt to remove such extraneous material as lignin, which binds cellulose together in a tree. (Wood consists of 25–30 percent lignin and about 45 percent cellulose.) A high percentage of lignin, which is unstable and yields various acids as it degrades, is the primary reason that so much mid-nineteenth-century groundwood paper is brittle, discolored, and weak. It is also why some modern papers used in newspapers and inexpensive paperback books deteriorate so quickly. Today a longer-lasting paper is made by chemically treating the wood fibers to remove lignin and other impurities. Paper made from chemical wood pulp is not as vulnerable to acid degradation as that made from groundwood pulp, but it is by no means acid free. Residual chemicals from the manufacturing process provide fuel for future acid formation.

Although acid hydrolysis accounts for most paper deterioration,[3] environmental factors influence the acids produced and the rate at which degrading chemical reactions occur. The most important environmental factors are temperature, humidity, light, and air pollution.

Humidity, the presence of moisture in the air,[4] affects paper in several ways. Paper, like leather, vellum, glue, paste, gelatin emulsions, and other materials comprising library and archives collections are hygroscopic, capable of giving up moisture or absorbing it according to the relative humidity of the surrounding air. In a dry environment, paper gives up moisture to the surrounding air and its flexibility is reduced, causing fibers to break more easily. The glue, cloth, leather, vellum, and other components of books can be similarly affected. On the other hand, at higher relative humidity levels, the increased moisture content accelerates deteriorative chemical reactions. High humidity, especially when combined with high temperatures, encourages the growth of mold and mildew and increases the possibility of insect infestation.

A potentially more damaging consequence of humidity is the dimensional change that occurs as paper and other archival materials respond repeatedly to fluctuating humidity. As the relative humidity rises, hygroscopic materials swell; as it falls, they shrink, causing warping, splitting and breaking of fibers. Although this movement may not be visible to the naked eye, the resulting internal physical stress and dimensional instability can be damaging.

Fluctuation of temperature is not as harmful as fluctuation of humidity, but it also adversely affects material. Since relative humidity is dependent upon temperature, in most cases a temperature change causes a change in relative humidity. A small change in temperature causes a greater change in relative humidity. If the temperature of a room at 51 percent relative humidity increases from 70°F to 72°F, the relative humidity decreases by 6 percent. A temperature increase causes moisture-absorbent materials to swell, but that response is small compared with the change that results from the accompanying humidity change. To state it another way, the same amount of expansion occurs from either a 4 percent rise in relative humidity or a 10°C rise in temperature.[5]

As the temperature rises, the rate of chemical activity in organic materials increases. A 10°C increase in temperature approximately doubles the rate of chemical activity. Scientific tests indicate that the life of paper can be doubled by reducing the temperature by 10°F.

Composite objects like books contain various materials which may respond at different rates to changes in temperature and relative humidity. These varying responses can initiate a complex set of conflicting internal forces which causes severe structural damage.

Light affects archival material by inducing deteriorative chemical reaction. When energy in the form of light is absorbed by paper, it "excites" the molecules, making them behave more energetically. The excited molecules may appear as heat, which increases the rate of chemical activity, or they may catalyze other chemical reactions. On newspaper, light acts as a catalyst initiating reactions between lignin and other compounds causing the paper to darken. The fading of colored inks and paper is another common manifestation of photochemical deterioration.

Although all light is potentially damaging, ultraviolet light is most dangerous because its wavelength is shorter and therefore more energetic. Light in the middle of the ultraviolet range (which is invisible) has a damage factor of 145 times that of green light, which is in the middle of the visible spectrum.[6] Sunlight and fluorescent lighting are two common sources rich in ultraviolet radiation. Conversely, incandescent lighting, which has virtually no ultraviolet radiation, produces infrared radiation (heat).

The damaging effect of light is cumulative. The degree of damage caused by light is a product of wavelength, intensity (usually measured in footcandles), and length of exposure. A brief exposure under a bright light can be just as damaging as extended exposure under a low light level. Even more disturbing, the chemical reactions initiated by light continue even after an object has been withdrawn from the light and placed in darkness.

Air pollution is another enemy of archival material. Dust is not only aesthetically annoying, it is an abrasive, and when mixed with perspiration and skin oils can create permanent stains. Very fine dust particulates can absorb gaseous pollutants like sulfur dioxide (this is known as *acid dust*) and become embedded in the fibers of book and paper materials. Mold growth is also facilitated by dust.

The most serious atmospheric pollutants are gaseous: sulfur dioxide, ozone, oxides of nitrogen. Catalyzed by atmospheric humidity, sulfur dioxide reacts both in the air and on the surface of paper to form sulfuric acid. High humidity and ultraviolet light speed the reaction. Paper with high lignin content is especially vulnerable because it absorbs sulfuric acid more readily than other papers. This phenomenon can be seen in paperback books whose exposed edges are browner and more brittle where the sulfur dioxide has diffused than toward the interior of the book.

Ozone, a powerful oxidant, is a threat to almost all organic material. Produced naturally in the upper atmosphere, it is found in urban areas in abnormal concentrations as photochemical smog, the result of sunlight on automotive exhaust gases.

Oxides of nitrogen are oxidizing agents which also appear in high concentrations in urban areas. They form nitric acid, which in turn promotes acid hydrolysis. A study conducted in 1977 showed that ozone and nitrogen oxides freely entered the National Archives building in Washington through the ventilating system. A direct correlation was found between external and internal concentrations. The highest levels both inside and outside the Archives occurred during the morning and evening rush hours. The concentrations were lowest between 2:00 A.M. and 5:00 A.M.[7]

Preservation Strategies: Controlling the Environment

The structural breakdown of paper results from complex interrelated chemical reactions which are governed by a variety of external and internal factors. The basic strategy for preserving and maintaining the useful life of paper involves control of the factors which cause the destruction of cellulose and the other components of research material. Since temperature, humidity, light, and air quality have a pervasive impact on the degradation rate of organic materials, controlling the environment is one of the most effective preservation approaches.

All chemical reactions are slowed by a decrease in temperature. As stated earlier, a 10°F reduction in temperature can double the life of paper. Although it is reasonable to assume that the colder the temperature, the longer archival collections will last, archival collections do not exist in isolation and a compromise must be made between temperature and the physical circumstances of the collections. If the collection is housed in reading areas where researchers use the material, a temperature compatible with human comfort must be maintained. Given this situation, preservation specialists agree that a $67° \pm 2°F$ is a reasonable temperature compromise for a space which must accommodate both people and archival material.

The decision to maintain separate areas for storage of collections must take into account the possible consequences. One danger in maintaining dissimilar environments for storage and use is cycling, the alternate expansion and contraction of materials as they are transported from one environment to another. Even though cycling changes may not be visible, they occur at a molecular level. Bound volumes may undergo even greater stress, because not only do they respond rapidly to abrupt environmental change, but they are simultaneously flexed during use. Another danger is the possible formation of condensation on material carried from a much cooler room into a warmer one.

Control of humidity is even more crucial than control of temperature because deteriorative chemical reactions are facilitated by the presence of moisture, embrittlement results from lack of moisture, microbiological growth is encouraged by too much moisture, and organic material responds more drastically to changes in relative humidity than to changes in temperature. The optimal humidity level for the storage and use of archival collections should be determined by the format of the materials. Recognizing that low humidity slows chemical reactions, the humidity level should be determined by the amount of flexibility loss that is acceptable. In a collection where unbound manuscripts and single-leaf items prevail, a lower humidity and loss of flexibility may be acceptable, but bound material which must be flexed during use requires a higher humidity to prevent damage. A humidity level as low as 25 percent might be appropriate for collections of unbound manuscripts, but for collections containing a variety of formats and materials, a level of 45 percent ±3 percent is a recommended compromise. Vellum should ideally have a higher humidity level of up to 55 percent.

Even more important than the specific temperature and humidity levels is controlling the fluctuation of those levels. A stable environment at less than ideal temperature and humidity is preferable to fluctuating levels that cannot be controlled. The cycling in temperature and humidity caused by turning off fan units each night contributes significantly to the deterioration of archival collections. Good air circulation eliminates stagnant air pockets which may result in microclimates of undesirable environmental conditions.

The damaging effects of light are minimized by limiting intensity and length of exposure and by selecting lighting sources carefully. Storage spaces should be kept dark when not in use, and individual aisles and sections of rooms should have separate light controls. Task lights and desk lamps should always be turned off when not in use. In areas where collections and users coexist, the overall light level should be kept as low as work efficiency will allow. Individual work areas can be equipped with supplemental task lighting, reducing the necessity for a high level of ambient light.

Every attempt should be made to eliminate ultraviolet light. In addition to shades and blinds, windows can be equipped with clear ultraviolet filters. Windows in storage areas should be permanently blocked or painted over. Fluorescent ceiling and desk lamps can be fitted with fairly inexpensive ultraviolet filtering "sleeves."

In addition to sunlight and fluorescent lighting, sources rich in ultraviolet include high-intensity metal halide and quartz lighting. As general guidelines, incandescent lighting should be used wherever possible, the light level should be as low as practical for the activity taking place, and lights should be extinguished when they are not needed. In areas where items of permanent value are used and stored, a staff member should routinely monitor the level and ultraviolet content of lighting.

Control of air quality is generally a function of the heating, ventilating, and air conditioning systems. Filters are used to trap particulate matter and eliminate gaseous pollutants. Electrostatic precipitators are not recommended for use in libraries or archives because they produce ozone.

Housekeeping is another environmental factor with preservation implications. A clean, neat environment discourages insects and rodents. Orderly, organized areas present fewer fire hazards. Eating, drinking, and smoking (if allowed) should be confined to designated areas which are frequently cleaned. Although chemical pesticides are commonly used in libraries and archives, meticulous housekeeping reduces the need for noxious chemicals. Psychologically, a neat, clean environment projecting an image of concern can set the tone for careful use of research material.

Use and Preservation

It is ironic that although use by readers is the very reason for preservation efforts, handling can be the worse enemy of archival material. It is imperative that researchers recognize the vulnerability of the materials and make deliberate efforts to minimize the hazards of use. Preservation begins with acquisition procedures and continues through reshelving after use. Proper handling and storage techniques enter into all activities affecting archival collections, including use by the researcher.

Storage techniques can significantly slow the deteriorative processes. Because the chemical content is a major factor in paper's rate of deterioration, and because acid in paper can migrate, it is essential that file folders, manuscript boxes, and other storage materials not be acid-producing themselves. A variety of commercially available acid-free "archival quality" products is available for storing paper-based materials. Free of groundwood, lignin, and other potentially harmful chemicals and additives, these are paper products made from wood pulp (not rags as is commonly believed) which has been chemically bleached to remove highly reactive noncellulose ingredients. An alkaline size is used in place of alum, and an alkaline buffer such as calcium carbonate neutralizes future acid attack, whether from the paper's own deterioration or from acid migration from adjacent paper.

Acid-free buffered paper and board should always be used for prolonged contact with archival collections, with the exception of some types of photographic materials, for which the use of a acid-free but unbuffered paper is preferable. Buffering agents may adversely affect some types of photographic prints.

Shelving for archival material should be of a suitable size for the type of material it supports. Large items should be shelved flat, fully supported rather than upright. Large volumes should not be stacked more than three volumes high to avoid crushing the lower volumes. Bookends should be used for materials stored upright but they should not pinch the items they support. Archival materials should always be stored on smooth, nondamaging surfaces, such as steel with a baked enamel finish. Wood is not satisfactory for shelving because of the acids which it exudes; in addition, varnishes and finishes used on wood may give off harmful vapors.

The arrangement of an archival collection has preservation implications which may not be immediately apparent to researchers. A well-planned arrangement based on the projected use of the collection increases the efficiency of research and minimizes unnecessary handling. Missing materials are quickly identified in a well-arranged collection. Thorough, precise collection descriptions and finding aids facilitate identification of pertinent materials without requiring perusal of an entire collection. An efficiently arranged archival collection separates different types of material; each format is shelved together to eliminate the problems resulting from shelving different sizes and shapes side by side.

As archival collections are processed and arranged, material may be found to be too valuable or fragile to be used in its original form. Access may be restricted and microfilm or photocopy reproductions provided. It is not uncommon for institutions to protect heavily used material in this way. Using a microfilm or photocopy may not be as convenient or provide the same thrill to a researcher as using the original, but it is often the wisest means of ensuring the survival of unique and valuable items. To the researcher, perhaps the most obvious consequences of deteriorated paper, apart from the telltale "cornflakes" on shelves and in manuscript boxes, is having to use research material which has been reformatted to save its content. For most material, this has meant microfilming. Research is being conducted on the suitability of alternative formats, such as magnetic tape and optical disk, but questions about long-term stability and future availability of the required hardware (which becomes outdated almost on a daily basis) have kept them from becoming a viable alternative to microfilm. The Committee on Preservation of Historical Records of the National Research Council states that the media

> appropriate for archival preservation are paper and photographic film. . . . Materials and technical problems inherent in the use of magnetic and optical storage media and the lack of suitable standards for archival quality make their use as preservation media for archival storage inappropriate at the present time.[8]

Microforms (film and fiche) are subject to the same deteriorating influences as paper. Photographic film, which is not inherently stable, deteriorates in time, and the gelatin emulsion on photographic materials is susceptible to attack by fungi and microorganisms.

To ensure the survival of the contents of a valuable book or collection, preservation microfilming often includes the production of several copies: a positive copy for use by readers; a negative copy (sometimes called a *service negative* or *reproduction negative*) from which additional copies are made as needed; and a master negative (preservation master) which is stored in a separate, closely controlled environment which may be a secure off-site underground storage vault. The importance of proper processing and storage of preservation masters is intensified by the fact that they may be the sole surviving carriers of their contents. Preservation masters should be stored in an environment where the temperature does not exceed 68°F, with the relative humidity between 30 and 40 percent, and the air free of pollutants. Suitable film stock is essential for the longevity of preservation masters. Black-and-white silver halide film on a safety base (usually polyester) is recommended. Standards specifying maximum levels of residual processing chemicals have been established to minimize self-generating deterioration.

Photocopying is one of the most damaging uses to which a book can be subjected. Books are not designed to be flattened out under pressure. Fragile bindings may break when an open book is pressed flat on a copy machine in an attempt to capture all of the text in the gutter margin, and even strong bindings gradually weaken with repeated copying. If the pages are brittle, there is danger of text loss as the paper breaks and chips. Photocopying fold-out maps, illustrations, and charts is even riskier because the book must be supported and the unfolded extension maneuvered into place on the copy machine. Even photocopying flat, single-leaf items presents a risk. On some photocopiers the paper can become snagged at the edge of the glass and broken off. Another hazard is the cover on the copying surface. When the cover, whether flexible or rigid, is lifted, a single sheet can cling to it and be damaged.

A responsible researcher only approaches photocopying after screening research materials carefully to select what is absolutely necessary for copying. On many occasions a few handwritten notes can be a completely adequate substitute. Many libraries and archives restrict photocopying of rare, valuable, and fragile materials, fold-outs, and large items. In some institutions copying is performed only by trained staff members. Microfilming or photography is sometimes suggested or specified to researchers who need copies of rare and fragile materials. A photocopy machine may soon be available that will cradle a book and copy it from above to eliminate having to turn it upside down and open it flat.

Awareness of the precarious state of so much of our written history has grown considerably in the past few years. Cooperative efforts are being planned and implemented at local, state, regional, and national levels to save as many materials as possible. Not everything will survive. Researchers of today can significantly influence the resources available for future research by serving as advocates for preservation issues, by contributing to the intellectual process of selection, and by using research materials responsibly.

NOTES
AND BIBLIOGRAPHIES

Notes to 1. *Introduction to Archival Research*

1. Leopold von Ranke, "Introduction to the *History of the Latin and Teutonic Nations*," in *The Secret of World History: Selected Writings on the Art and Science of History,* ed. and trans. Roger Wines (New York: Fordham University Press, 1981), 58.

2. John Walton Caughey, *Hubert Howe Bancroft: Historian of the West* (Berkeley and Los Angeles: University of California Press, 1946), 80–81, 350–65.

3. Donald R. McCoy, *The National Archives: America's Ministry of Documents, 1934–1968* (Chapel Hill: University of North Carolina Press, 1978), 3–12; Victor Gondos, *J. Franklin Jameson and the Birth of the National Archives, 1906–1926* (Philadelphia: University of Pennsylvania Press, 1981).

4. "Paid Civilian Employment of the Federal Government: 1816 to 1970," *Historical Statistics of the United States,* (Washington: U.S. Bureau of the Census, 1975), 1103; "Federal Civilian Employment—Summary: 1970 to 1984," *Statistical Abstract of the United States: 1986,* (Washington: U.S. Bureau of the Census, 1985), 322.

5. Fred Somkin, review of *Postmortem: New Evidence in the Case of Sacco and Vanzetti,* by William Young and David E. Kaiser, *American Historical Review* 91 (October 1986): 1011–12.

6. U.S. Department of State. *Foreign Relations of the United States* (Washington: Government Printing Office, 1861–   ).

7. Allen Nevins, *The Gateway to History,* rev. ed. (Chicago: Quadrangle Books, 1963), 183–84.

8. Ibid., 183.

9. Great Britain. Public Record Office. *Calendar of the Letters and*

Papers, Foreign and Domestic, of the Reign of Henry VIII (London: H. M. Stationery Office, 1862–1910).

10. G. R. Elton, *The Practice of History* (New York: Thomas Y. Crowell, 1967), 68–69.

11. Barbara W. Tuchman, *Practicing History: Selected Essays* (New York: Alfred A. Knopf, 1981), 20–21.

12. *The Letters of Henry Adams,* vol. 2, *1868–1885,* ed. J. C. Levenson et al. (Cambridge: Belknap Press of Harvard University Press, 1982), Adams to James Russell Lowell, 13 September 1879, 24 September 1879, and 10 October 1879; *The Letters of Mrs. Henry Adams, 1865–1882,* ed. Ward Thoron (Boston: Little, Brown, 1936), M. Adams to Pater [Robert William Hooper], 30 November 1879.

13. John Barker, *The Superhistorians: Makers of Our Past* (New York: Charles Scribner's Sons, 1982), 153–54.

14. Merton L. Dillon, *Ulrich Bonnell Phillips: Historian of the Old South* (Baton Rouge: Louisiana State University Press, 1985), 122–27; C. Vann Woodward, *Thinking Back: The Perils of Writing History* (Baton Rouge: Louisiana State University Press, 1986), 21–42; Ralph Blumenthal, "Boss Tweed's Unearthed Records May Shed Light on City Chicanery," *New York Times,* 10 November 1972, pp. 41, 48.

15. Thomas Lask, "Success of Search for 'Roots' Leaves Alex Haley Surprised," *New York Times,* 23 November 1976, p. 40; Paul D. Zimmerman, review of *Roots,* by Alex Haley, *Newsweek,* 27 September 1976, 94–96.

16. A good general introduction is Donald Jackson, *The Story of Writing* (New York: Taplinger Publishing/Parker Pen Co., 1981). Examples of more specialized works are Charles Johnson and Hilary Jenkinson, *English Court Hand,* A.D. *1066 to 1500* (New York: Frederick Ungar, 1967) and L. C. Hector, *The Handwriting of English Documents,* 2d ed. (London: Edward Arnold, 1966).

17. Tuchman, *Practicing History,* 76–77.

18. One of the best known is Jacques Barzun and Henry Graff, *The Modern Researcher,* 4th ed. (New York: Harcourt Brace Jovanovich, 1985). Nevins, *Gateway to History,* is less practical in its orientation but treats essential issues in historical thinking.

19. Nevins, *Gateway to History,* 44–45.

20. Barzun and Graff, *Modern Researcher,* 125.

21. Elton, *Practice of History,* 76.

22. Nevins, *Gateway to History,* 152–53.

23. Ibid., 137–88.

24. Derek Shorrocks, County Archivist, to Margaret F. Stieg, 12 November 1986. See *Dictionary of National Biography* article on John Payne Collier.

25. Tuchman, *Practicing History,* 62.

Notes to *2. What Every Researcher Should Know about Arch.ves*

1. Theodore R. Schellenberg, *The Management of Archives* (New York: Columbia University Press, 1965). Schellenberg's terms will be referred to throughout the chapter. This basic work provides additional information for the interested beginning researcher.

2. Michael Stephen Hindus, Theodore R. Hammett, and Barbara M. Hobson, *The Files of the Massachus Superior Court, 1859–1959: An Analysis and a Plan for Action* (Boston: G. K. Hall, 1980).

3. Library of Congress. Descriptive Cataloging Division. *National Union Catalog of Manuscript Collections* (Hamden, CT: Shoe String Press, 1962–   ).

Bibliography for *5. Archival Reference Tools*

American Geographical Society. *Index to Maps in Books and Periodicals.* Boston: G. K. Hall, 1968.

Benjamin, Mary. *Autographs: A Key to Collecting.* Rev. ed. New York: Dover, 1986.

Berkeley, Edmund, Jr., ed. *Autographs and Manuscripts: A Collector's Manual.* New York: Charles Scribner's Sons, 1978.

The Biographical Directory of the American Congress, 1774–1971. Washington: Government Printing Office, 1971.

Biography and Genealogy Master Index. Edited by Miranda C. Herbert and Barbara McNeil. 2d ed. Detroit: Gale Research Co., 1980.

Cahoon, Herbert, Thomas V. Lange, and Charles Ryskamp. *American Literary Autographs, from Washington Irving to Henry James.* New York: Dover, 1977.

Carrington, David K., and Richard R. Stephenson. *Map Collections in the United States and Canada: A Directory.* New York: Special Libraries Association, 1978.

Dictionary of American Biography. New York: Scribner, 1928–   .

Duckett, Kenneth W. *Modern Manuscripts: A Practical Manual for Their Management, Care and Use.* Nashville: American Association for State and Local History, 1975.

Eakle, Arlene, and John Cerny. *The Source: A Guidebook of American Genealogy.* Salt Lake City: Ancestry Publishing Co., 1984.

Evans, Max, and Lisa B. Webber. *MARC for Archives and Manuscripts: A Compendium of Practice.* Madison: State Historical Society of Wisconsin, 1985.

Freidel, Frank, ed. *Harvard Guide to American History.* Rev. ed. Cambridge: Belknap Press of Harvard University Press, 1974.

Gravell, Thomas L. *A Catalogue of American Watermarks, 1690–1835.* New York: Garland, 1979.

———. *A Catalogue of Foreign Watermarks Found on Paper Used in America, 1700–1835.* New York: Garland, 1983.

Hamilton, Charles. *American Autographs: Signers of the Declaration of Independence, Revolutionary War Leaders, Presidents.* 2 vols. Norman: University of Oklahoma Press, 1983.

———. *Collecting Autographs and Manuscripts.* Norman: University of Oklahoma Press, 1961.

———. *The Signature of America: A Fresh Look at Famous Handwriting.* New York: Harper and Row, 1979.

Henson, Stephen L. *Archives, Personal Papers, and Manuscripts.* Washington: Manuscript Division, Library of Congress, 1983.

Jones, H. G. *Local Government Records: An Introduction to Their Management, Preservation, and Use.* Nashville: American Association for State and Local History, 1980.

Kaminkow, Marion J. *A Complement to Genealogies in the Library of Congress.* Baltimore: Magna Carta Books, 1981.

———. *Genealogies in the Library of Congress: A Bibliography.* Baltimore: Magna Carta Books, 1972.

Kaminkow, Marion J., ed. *United States Local Histories in the Library of Congress: A Bibliography*. 4 vols. Baltimore: Magna Carta Books, 1975.

Kane, Lucile M. *A Guide to the Care and Administration of Manuscripts*. 2d ed. Nashville: American Association for State and Local History, 1966.

Middleton, Arthur P., and Douglass Adair. "The Mystery of the Horn Papers," *William and Mary Quarterly*, 3d ser., 4 (1947): 409–45.

New York Public Library. Research Libraries. *Dictionary Catalog of the Map Division*. Boston: G. K. Hall, 1971.

Rapport, Leonard. "Fakes and Facsimiles: Problems of Identification." *American Archivist* 42 (January 1979): 13–58.

Sahli, Nancy. *MARC for Archives and Manuscripts: The AMC Format*. Chicago: Society of American Archivists, 1985.

Sealock, Richard Burl. *Bibliography of Place-Name Literature in the United States, Canada, Alaska, and Newfoundland*. 3d ed. Chicago: American Library Association, 1982.

Simon, John Y. "In Search of Margaret Johnson Erwin: A Research Note." *Journal of American History* 69 (March 1983): 932–41. See also the response to Simon, pp. 942–45 and further comment in the June 1983 issue, pp. 224–26.

Spear, Dorothea A. *Bibliography of American Directories through 1860*. Barre, MA: Barre Publishers for the American Antiquarian Society, 1961.

Stryker-Rodda, Harriet. *Understanding Colonial Handwriting*. Rev. ed. Baltimore: Genealogical Publishing Co., 1986.

Taylor, Priscilla S., ed. *Manuscripts: The First Twenty Years*. Westport, CT: Greenwood, 1984.

U.S. National Archives. *Guide to Genealogical Research in the National Archives*. Washington: National Archives and Records Service, 1982.

BASIC MANUALS OF THE SOCIETY OF AMERICAN ARCHIVISTS

Brichford, Maynard. *Archives and Manuscripts: Appraisal and Accessioning*. Chicago: Society of American Archivists, 1977.

Casterline, Gail Farr. *Archives and Manuscripts: Exhibits*. Chicago: Society of American Archivists, 1980.

Ehrenberg, Ralph E. *Archives and Manuscripts: Maps and Architectural Drawings*. Chicago: Society of American Archivists, 1982.

Fleckner, John. *Archives and Manuscripts: Surveys*. Chicago: Society of American Archivists, 1977.

Gracy, David B. *Archives and Manuscripts: Arrangement and Description*. Chicago: Society of American Archivists, 1977.

Headstrom, Margaret L. *Archives and Manuscripts: Machine-Readable Records*. Chicago: Society of American Archivists, 1984.

Hickerson, H. Thomas. *Archives and Manuscripts: An Introduction to Automated Access*. Chicago: Society of American Archivists, 1981.

Hobert, Sue E. *Archives and Manuscripts: Reference and Access*. Chicago: Society of American Archivists, 1977.

Pederson, Anne E., and Gail Farr Casterline. *Archives and Manuscripts: Public Programs*. Chicago: Society of American Archivists, 1982.

Peterson, Gary M., and Trudy Huskamp Peterson. *Archives and Manuscripts: Law*. Chicago: Society of American Archivists, 1985.

Ritzenthaler, Mary Linn. *Archives and Manuscripts: Conservation*. Chicago: Society of American Archivists, 1983.

Ritzenthaler, Mary Linn, Gerald J. Munoff, and Margery S. Long. *Archives and Manuscripts: Administration of Photograph Collections*. Chicago: Society of American Archivists, 1984.

Sung, Carolyn Hoover. *Archives and Manuscripts: Reprography*. Chicago: Society of American Archivists, 1982.

Walch, Timothy. *Archives and Manuscripts: Security*. Chicago: Society of American Archivists, 1977.

Notes to *6. Business Records*

1. Jean Cucia, "Managing Media and Resources," *Information Management* 10 (May 1984): 12–14.

2. T. R. Schellenberg, *The Management of Archives* (New York: Columbia University Press, 1965), 126–28.

3. Florence Bartoshesky, "Business Records at the Harvard Business School," *Business History Review* 59 (Autumn 1985): 475–83.

4. Meyer Fishbein, "Business Archives," in *Encyclopedia of Library and Information Science* (New York: Marcel Dekker, 1968), 3:520–22.

5. David R. Smith, "An Historical Look at Business Archives," *American Archivist* 45 (September 1982): 273–78.

6. Lawrence Vail Coleman, *Company Museums* (Washington, D.C.: American Association of Museums, 1943).

7. *Directory of Business Archives in the United States and Canada* (Chicago: Society of American Archivists, 1980). A new survey of business archives programs is currently underway with publication anticipated for 1988. Interested researchers should contact the Society of American Archivists, 600 South Federal Street, Suite 504, Chicago, Illinois 60605 for details.

8. Victor J. Danilov, "Museum Pieces," *Public Relations Journal* 42 (August 1986): 14.

9. National Historical Publications and Records Commission. *Directory of Archives and Manuscript Repositories in the United States* (Washington, D.C.: National Archives and Records Service, 1979); Betty Pease Smith, ed., *Directory of Historical Agencies in North America* (Nashville: American Association for State and Local History, 1986); *National Inventory of Documentary Sources in the United States* (Alexandria, VA: Chadwyck-Healey, 1984); U.S. Library of Congress, *National Union Catalog of Manuscript Collections* (Hamden, CT: Shoe String Press, 1962–).

10. Two of the best-detailed guides are *Guide to the Archives and Research Library* (Dearborn, MI: The Edison Institute, Henry Ford Museum and Greenfield Village, 1983) and Robert W. Lovette, *List of Business Manuscripts in Baker Library,* 2d ed. (Cambridge: Harvard University Press, 1951).

11. Probably the most comprehensive collection of corporate histories is the excellent series of monographs produced under the auspices of the History Department of the Wells Fargo Bank. It provides detailed historical analyses of the bank's operations throughout the western United States.

12. Two good examples of corporate histories produced by outside researchers are W. David Lewis and Wesley Phillips New-

ton, *Delta: The History of an Airline* (Athens, GA: University of Georgia Press, 1979) and Wayne C. Broehl, Jr., *John Deere's Company: A History of Deere and Its Times* (New York: Doubleday, 1984).

Bibliography for 7. *Religious Records*

Field, W. N. "The Founding of an Archdiocesan Archive." *Catholic World* 57 (July–August 1985): 45–47.
Hannaford, Claudia, "Church and Synagogue Library Association: Fifteen Years of Ecumenical Concern for Quality Service in Religious Libraries." *Special Libraries* 74 (July 1983): 271–77.
Kohl, Rachel, and Rodda, Dorothy. *Church and Synagogue Library Resources*. 4th ed. Bryn Mawr, PA: Church and Synagogue Library Association, 1984.
Leary, W. "Methodist Archives." *Archives* 16 (April 1983): 16–27.
Ling, Evelyn R. *Archivists in the Church or Synagogue Library*. Bryn Mawr, PA: Church and Synagogue Library Association, 1981.
Marty, Martin E. "A Curious People—A Useable Past." *Concordia Historical Institute Quarterly* 58: (Fall 1985): 98–102.
Newton, LaVase. *The Church Library Handbook*. Rev. ed. Eugene, OR: Harvest House, 1978.
Powell, Ted F. "The Miracle of Microfilm: The Foundation of the Largest Genealogical Collection in the World." *Microform Review* 14 (Summer 1985): 148–56.
Suelflow, August. *Religious Archives, An Introduction*. Chicago: Society of American Archivists, 1980.

Notes to, and Bibliography for, 8. *Public Records*

NOTES

1. David E. Kyvig and Myron A. Marty, *Nearby History: Exploring the Past Around You* (Nashville: American Association for State

and Local History, 1982), 269–86. Regional branches of the National Archives, state archives, and state historical societies are listed with addresses.

2. H. G. Jones, *Local Government Records: An Introduction to Their Management, Preservation and Use* (Nashville: American Association for State and Local History, 1980), 107.

3. Ibid., 107–20. Jones recounts the development of local records systems in various parts of the United States.

4. Thomas E. Felt, *Researching, Writing, and Publishing Local History* (Nashville: American Association for State and Local History, 1976), 43.

BIBLIOGRAPHY

Armstrong, Robert D. "Beast in the Bathtub and other Archival Laments." *American Archivist* 45 (Fall 1982): 375–84.

Berner, Richard C. *Archival Theory and Practice in the United States.* Seattle: University of Washington Press, 1984.

———. "Manuscript Collections, Archives, and Special Collections: Their Relationships." *Library and Archival Security* 5 (Winter 1983): 9–17.

Birdsall, W. F. "Archivists, Librarians, and Issues during the Pioneering Era of the American Archival Movement." *Journal of Library History* 14 (Fall 1979): 457–79.

Brodie, C. "The Local Historian and the Local Archivist." *Special Libraries Association News* 186 (March–April 1985): 28–31.

Brooks, Philip C. *Research in Archives: The Use of Unpublished Primary Sources.* Chicago: University of Chicago Press, 1969.

Brumberg, G. David. "Sources and Uses of Local History Materials." *Bookmark* 39 (Winter 1981): 116–23.

Buchart, Ron. *Local Schools Exploring Their History.* Nashville: American Association for State and Local History, 1986.

Chandler, John. "Indexes for Local and Family History: A User's View." *Indexer* 13 (October 1983): 223–27.

Clary, David A. "Trouble is My Business: A Private View of Public History." *American Archivist* 44 (Spring 1981): 105–12.

Colorado State Archives. *Guidelines for the Preservation and Disposi-*

tion of Public Records. 2 vols. Denver: Colorado State Archives, 1975–76.

Crittenden, Christopher. "The Public Library and Local Historical Sources." *History News* 30 (July 1975): 69–70.

Felt, Thomas E. *Researching, Writing, and Publishing Local History.* Nashville: American Association for State and Local History, 1976.

Gardner, James B., and George Rollie Adams. *Ordinary People and Everyday Lives.* Nashville: American Association for State and Local History, 1980.

Hesseltine, William, and Donald R. McNeil, eds. *In Support of Clio.* Madison: University of Wisconsin Press, 1958.

Hoy, Suellen M., and Michael C. Robinson, eds. *Public Works History in the United States: A Guide to the Literature.* Nashville: American Association for State and Local History, 1982.

Jacobsen, Edna L. "State and Local Government Archives." *Library Trends* 5 (January 1957): 397–405.

Jones, H. G. *Local Government Records: An Introduction to Their Management, Preservation and Use.* Nashville: American Association for State and Local History, 1980.

———. "Pink Elephant Revisited." *American Archivist* 43 (Fall 1980): 473–80.

———. *The Records of a Nation: Their Management, Preservation and Use.* New York: Atheneum, 1969.

Jordan, Philip D. "In Search of Local Legal Records." *American Archivist* 33 (October 1970): 379.

Kammen, Carol. *A Guide for Local Historians.* Nashville: American Association for State and Local History, 1986.

Kyvig, David E., and Myron A. Marty. *Nearby History: Exploring the Past Around You.* Nashville: American Association for State and Local History, 1982.

Miller, Nancy. "Public Access to Public Records: Some Threatening Reforms." *Wilson Library Bulletin* 56 (October 1981): 95–99.

Mitchell, Thornton W. *Norton on Archives: The Writings of Margaret Cross Norton on Archival and Records Management.* Chicago: Society of American Archivists, 1975.

Parker, Donald D. *Local History: How to Gather It, Write It, and Publish It.* Westport CT: Greenwood Press, 1979.

Posner, Ernest. *American State Archives.* Chicago: University of Chicago Press, 1964.

————. *Modern Archives, Principles and Techniques.* Chicago: University of Chicago Press, 1956.

Rendell, Kenneth W. "Ownership of Papers of Public Officials." *A B Bookman's Weekly* 73 (February 4, 1985): 70–74.

Tarahan, S. L. "Local History as an Information Service." *Bookmark* 41 (Winter 1983): 106–9.

Thompson, Enid T. "Commentary on Archival Management and Special Libraries." *Special Libraries* 69 (December 1978): 491–92. See also comment by F. Gerald Ham in *Special Libraries* 70 (November 1979): 7A.

————. *Local History Collections.* Nashville: American Association for State and Local History, 1978.

Bibliography for *10. Oral Histories*

ORAL HISTORY BIBLIOGRAPHIES

These bibliographies include books and articles about oral history or using oral history. They will guide the researcher to oral history collections in many fields.

Anderson, R. Wayne. "Oral History Dissertations, 1977–1981." *Oral History Review* 10 (1982): 133–44.

————. "Oral History Dissertations, 1980–1982, and Masters Theses, 1977–1982." *Oral History Review* 11 (1983): 125–29.

Fox, John J. "Bibliography Up-Date." *Oral History Review* 5 (1977): 125–29.

————. "Windows on the Past: A Guide to Oral History." *Choice* 17 (June 1980): 495–508.

Havlice, Patricia Pate. *Oral History: A Reference Guide and Annotated Bibliography.* Jefferson, NC: McFarland and Co., 1985. This very useful bibliography has entries on manuals, articles about oral history, guides to collections, and books based on oral history.

A well-done subject index enables users to find publications on their topic. The researcher should start here.

Stenberg, Henry G. "Selected Bibliography, 1977–1981." *Oral History Review* 10 (1982): 119–32.

Stephenson, Shirley E. "Selected Bibliography, 1980–1982." *Oral History Review* 11 (1983): 109–24.

———. "Selected Bibliography, 1982–1983." *Oral History Review* 12 (1984): 119–41.

———. "Selected Bibliography, 1983–1984." *Oral History Review* 13 (1985): 102–18.

Waserman, Manfred J. *Bibliography on Oral History*. rev ed. N.Y.: Oral History Association, 1975. A 400-entry bibliography which includes catalogs of outstanding collections. Subject index.

ORAL HISTORY—GENERAL

This section lists works on oral historiography, considerations of the appropriate uses of oral history, and evaluations of the reliability of oral history.

Allen, Barbara, and Lynwood Montell. *From Memory to History: Using Oral Sources in Local Historical Research*. Nashville: American Association for State and Local History, 1981. Evaluation of oral history and its use in writing history.

Brady, John. *The Craft of Interviewing*. Cincinnati, Ohio: Writers Digest Books, 1976. A breezy book on various interviewing techniques, many of which are not suitable for oral history, although full of ideas both good and bad on how to obtain the information.

Dunaway, David K., and Willa K. Baum. *Oral History: An Interdisciplinary Anthology*. Nashville: American Association for State and Local History, 1984. A collection of the best scholarly writing on oral history, its uses, promise, and problems. Not a manual, but the full bibliographies following each chapter are a key to all writings on oral history up to 1983.

Moss, William W. *Oral History Program Manual*. New York: Praeger, 1974. Thoughtful consideration of how to set up a large-scale project, based on the experiences of the John F. Kennedy Oral History Program. This is essential reading for the serious, scholarly researcher-oral historian.

Neuenschwander, John A. *Oral History and the Law*. Lexington, KY: Oral History Association, 1985. The latest and clearest statement of legal considerations for oral history, by a past president of the Oral History Association who is also a professor of history and a copyright lawyer.

Oral History Association. *Evaluation Guidelines*. Lexington, KY: Oral History Association, 1980. A brief booklet encapsulating the ethics and standards of the oral history community.

Seldon, Anthony, and Joanna Pappworth. *By Word of Mouth*. New York: Methuen, 1983. A valuable book on undertaking archival oral histories with key persons in politics, science, and the arts. Includes case studies and comments on legal considerations.

Stielow, Frederick J. *The Management of Oral History Sound Archives*. Westport, CT: Greenwood Press, 1986

Thompson, Paul. *The Voice of the Past: Oral History*. New York: Oxford University Press, 1978. A theoretical and practical guide to oral history by England's leading oral historian, and the best book thus far on oral historiography.

GUIDES TO ORAL HISTORY—National, Subject, Regional, and Collections

This section cites representative oral history guides. By searching local online data bases for these guides by title or author and inspecting the full entry, the researcher can often determine which key words to use to locate other oral history guides in the data base.

National Guides

Cook, Patsy. *Directory of Oral History Programs in the United States*. Sanford, NC: Microfilming Corporation of America, 1982.

Meckler, Alan M., and Ruth McMullin. *Oral History Collections*. New York: R. R. Bowker, 1975. A dictionary guide by subject and name of interviewee, providing convenient access for researchers.

Shumway, Gary L. *Oral History in the United States: A Directory*. New York: Oral History Association, 1971. The first national directory to list oral history programs by state, with an index to subject specialties. Old but still valuable.

In addition, a directory edited by Allen Smith, *Oral History Collections in the United States,* has been announced for late fall 1987 by Oryx Press. Periodic updating is planned to keep the information current.

Subject Guides

American Jewish Committee. *Catalog of Memoirs of the William Wiener Oral History Library.* New York: American Jewish Committee, 1978.

Archives of American Art. *The Card Catalog of the Oral History Collections of the Archives of American Art.* Wilmington, DE: Scholarly Resources, 1984.

Aspray, William, and Bruce Bruemmer. *Guide to the Oral History Collection of the Charles Babbage Institute.* Minneapolis: Center for the History of Information Processing, Charles Babbage Institute, 1986.

Dale, Doris Cruger. *A Directory of Oral History Tapes of Librarians in the United States and Canada.* Chicago: American Library Association, 1986.

DeGolyer Institute for American Studies. *Oral History Collection on the Performing Arts in America.* Dallas: Oral History Program, Southern Methodist University, 1984.

Frank, Benis M., comp. *Marine Corps Oral History Collection Catalog.* Washington, D.C.: History of Museums Division, Headquarters, U.S. Marine Corps, 1979.

Kendrick, Alice M., and Helen M. Knubel, eds. *The Oral History Collection of the Archives of Cooperative Lutheranism.* New York: Lutheran Council in the U.S.A., 1984.

Mann, Nancy D. "Directory of Women's Oral History Projects and Collections." *Frontiers: A Journal of Women Studies* 7, no. 2 (1983): 114–21.

Nowicke, Carol et al, eds. *Index of Oral Histories Relating to Naval Research and Development.* Bethesda, MD: David W. Taylor Naval Ship Research and Development Center, 1985.

Mikusko, M. Brady. *Preliminary Sourcebook of Oral Histories of Trade Union and Working Women in the United States.* Ann Arbor: Institute of Labor and Industrial Relations, University of Michigan, 1981.

South Dakota Oral History Center. *Index to the American Indian Research Project*. Pierre: South Dakota Oral History Center, 1979.

Regional and Collection Guides

California

Bullock, Constance S., comp. *The UCLA Oral History Program: Catalog of the Collection*. Los Angeles: Oral History Program, University of California, 1982.

Rafael, Ruth Kelson. *Western Jewish History Center: Guide to Archival and Oral History Collections*. Berkeley: Western Jewish History Center, Judah L. Magnes Memorial Museum, 1987.

Riess, Suzanne, and Willa K. Baum, eds. *Catalogue of the Regional Oral History Office, 1954–1979*. Berkeley: Bancroft Library, University of California, 1980.

San Luis Obispo County Oral History Organization. *History Comes Alive: Catalog of Oral History Holdings in San Luis Obispo County*. San Luis Obispo: San Luis Obispo County Oral History Organization, 1980.

Stephenson, Shirley S., ed. *Oral History Collections: California State University, Fullerton*. Fullerton: Oral History Program, California State University, 1985.

Colorado

Whistler, Nancy, comp. *Colorado Oral History Projects: A Directory*. Denver: Denver Public Library, 1977.

District of Columbia

Heintze, James R. *Scholars' Guide to Washington, D.C., for Audio Resources: Sound Recordings in the Arts, Humanities, and Social, Physical, and Life Sciences*. Washington, D.C.: Smithsonian Institution Press, 1985.

Hawaii

Catalog of Oral History Collections in Hawaii. Honolulu: Ethnic Studies Oral History Project, University of Hawaii, 1982.

Idaho

Buckendorf, Madeline, and Elizabeth P. Jacox, comps. and eds. *Directory of Oral History Resources*. Boise: Idaho Oral History Center, Idaho State Historical Society, 1982.

Latah County Museum Society, *Guide to the Latah County, Idaho*

Oral History Collection. Moscow, ID: Latah County Museum Society, 1977.

Illinois

Wrigley, Kathryn. *Directory of Illinois Oral History Resources.* Springfield, IL: Oral History Office, Sangamon State University, 1981.

Louisiana

Humphreys, Hubert. *Louisiana Oral History Collections: A Directory.* Shreveport: Louisiana State University, 1980.

Minnesota

Goff, Lila Johnson, and James Fogerty, comps. *The Oral History Collection of the Minnesota Historical Society.* St. Paul: Minnesota Historical Society, 1984.

New Jersey

Grele, Ronald, comp. *Oral History in New Jersey: A Directory.* Trenton: New Jersey Historical Commission, 1979.

New York

Mason, Elizabeth, and Louis M. Starr. *The Oral History Collection of Columbia University.* New York: Oral History Research Office, Columbia University, 1979.

Palmer, Joseph W., ed. *Directory of Oral History and Audio-Visual Local History Resources in Public Libraries in New York State.* Buffalo: School of Information and Library Studies, State University of New York, 1985.

Southwestern United States

Gallacher, Cathryn A. *Oral History Collections in the Southwest Region: a Directory and Subject Guide.* Accessible by computer, a detailed guide by subject and name of collection, regularly updated.

Texas

Jimenez, Rebecca Sharpless et al., eds. *Baylor University Institute for Oral History: A Guide to the Collections, 1970–85.* Waco: Baylor University, 1985.

North Texas State University Bulletin: Oral History Collection. Denton: North Texas State University, 1980.

Washington
Knight, Margot H. *Directory of Oral History in Washington State*. Pullman: Washington State University, 1981.

ORAL HISTORY MANUALS

These basic manuals will help the researcher who does not find a needed oral history and must create it him or herself. The researcher is urged to donate such oral histories to an appropriate archives or library.

Baum, Willa K. *Oral History for the Local Historical Society*. Nashville: American Association for State and Local History, 1987.

———. *Transcribing and Editing Oral History*. Nashville: American Association for State and Local History, 1977.

Charlton, Thomas L. *Oral History for Texans*. Austin: Texas Historical Commission, 1981. An excellent manual focusing on the history and concerns of a state, but the advice and bibliography are useful for all kinds of oral history.

Frontiers: A Journal of Women Studies 7, no. 1 (1983). A special issue containing articles on methods, uses, and examples of women's oral history projects. Sampling techniques, a listing of women's oral history projects, and a bibliography are included.

Handfield, F. Gerald, Jr. *History on Tape: A Guide for Oral History in Indiana*. Indianapolis: Indiana State Library, 1981. A brief, clear guide listing oral history projects in Indiana, with a time-line of the state's history.

Ives, Edward D. *The Tape-Recorded Interview: A Manual for Field Workers in Folklore and Oral History*. Knoxville: University of Tennessee Press, 1980. A comprehensive and readable manual by a leading folklorist, which is especially strong on recording techniques. Sample form letters, agreements, and accession forms are included.

Oblinger, Carl. *Interviewing the People of Pennsylvania*. Harrisburg: Pennsylvania Historical and Museum Commission, 1978. A work combining theory and method, with many clear examples.

O'Hanlan, Elizabeth. *Oral History for the Religious Archives: The Sinsinawa Collection*. Sinsinawa, WI: Sinsinawa Dominican Archives, 1978. Basic advice for any institutional archives, with good examples of a tape index and a program master index.

Reimer, Derek, David Mattison, and Allen W. Specht. *Voices, A Guide to Oral History*. Victoria, B.C.: British Columbia Provincial Archives, 1984. An excellent manual for producing radio-broadcast quality interviews, with detailed information on equipment and recording methods. Good examples of cataloging.

Whistler, Nancy. *Oral History Workshop Guide*. Denver: Colorado Center for Oral History, Denver Public Library, 1979. A well-organized manual for teaching oral history by means of a statewide workshop program.

Notes to, and Bibliography for, *11. Cartographic Sources*

NOTES

1. *Glossary of Technical Terms in Cartography* (London: The Royal Society, 1966), 25. The glossary was prepared by the Cartographic Subcommittee of the British National Committee for Geography.

2. *Glossary of Mapping, Charting, and Geodetic Terms*, 3d ed. (Washington: Defense Mapping Agency Topographic Center, 1973), 146.

3. Konstantin A. Kalishchev, "The Present Day Thematic Cartography and the Task of International Collaboration." Paper presented at the annual meeting of the International Geographic Union and International Cartographic Association, New Delhi, 1968.

4. International Cartographic Association, Commission II, *Multilingual Dictionary of Technical Terms in Cartography* (Wiesbaden: Franz Steiner, 1973), 40.

5. Clara Egli LeGear, comp., *United States Atlases: A List of National, State, City, and Regional Atlases in the Library of Congress*, vol. 1 (Washington: Library of Congress, 1950), iii.

6. Access to maps in selected books and periodicals is provided by *Current Geographical Publications* published by the American

Geographical Society Collection at the University of Wisconsin-Milwaukee.

BIBLIOGRAPHY

Abler, Ronald, and John S. Adams. *A Comparative Atlas of America's Great Cities: Twenty Metropolitan Regions.* Minneapolis: University of Minnesota Press for the Association of American Geographers, 1976.

Akrigg, G. P. V. "The Use of Maps in the Study of Place Names." *Association of Canadian Map Libraries Bulletin* 47 (June 1983): 18–25.

American Geographical Society. *Current Geographical Publications: Additions to the Research Catalogue of the American Geographical Society.* New York: American Geographical Society, vols. 1–41, no. 3, 1938–78. Milwaukee: American Geographical Society, vol. 41, no. 4–   , 1978–   .

—————. Map Department. *Index to Maps in Books and Periodicals.* 10 vols. Boston: G. K. Hall, 1968.

—————. *First Supplement.* Boston: G. K. Hall, 1971.

—————. *Second Supplement.* Boston: G. K. Hall, 1976.

Aronoff, Stanley. "The Map Accuracy Report: A User's View." *Photogrammetric Engineering and Remote Sensing* 48 (August 1982): 1309–12.

Barbour, Michael. "The Use of Maps: The Topographic and Thematic Traditions Contrasted." *Cartographic Journal* 20 (December 1983): 76–86.

Board, C., and R. M. Taylor. "Perception and Maps: Human Factors in Map Design." *Transactions,* n.s. 2 (1977): 19–36.

Conzen, Michael P. "The County Landownership Map in American: Its Commercial Development and Social Transformation, 1814–1939." *Imago Mundi* 36 (1984): 9–31.

Crone, Gerald R. "Modern Maps and Their Uses." In *Map Librarianship: Readings,* edited by Roman Drazniowsky, 163–72. Metuchen, NJ: Scarecrow Press, 1975.

Downs, Roger M., and David Stea. *Maps in Minds: Reflections on Cognitive Mapping.* New York: Harper & Row, 1977.

Greenwood, David. *Mapping.* 5th ed. Chicago: University of Chicago Press, 1971.

Harris, Chauncy D. *Bibliography of Geography: Introduction to General Aids.* Research paper no. 179. Chicago: University of Chicago, Department of Geography, 1976.

———. *Bibliography of Geography: The United States of America,* vol. 1. Research paper no. 206. Chicago: University of Chicago, Department of Geography, 1984.

Hodgkiss, Alan G. *Understanding Maps: A Systematic History of Their Use and Development.* Folkestone, England: Wm. Dawson & Son, 1981.

Hoehn, R. Philip. *Union List of Sanborn Fire Insurance Maps Held in Institutions in the United States and Canada.* 2 vols. Santa Cruz, CA: Western Association of Map Libraries, 1976–77.

Howard, James H., Jr., and Stephen M. Kerst. "Memory and Perception of Cartographic Information for Familiar and Unfamiliar Environments." *Human Factors* 23 (August 1981): 495–504.

Keates, John S. *Understanding Maps.* New York: Wiley and Sons, 1982.

Lohrentz, Ken. "Maps as Information Tools: A Neglected Resource." *Nebraska Library Association Quarterly* 13 (Winter 1982): 16–20.

Muehrcke, Phillip C. *Map Use, Reading, Analysis and Interpretation.* Madison, WI: J. P. Publications, 1978.

Ormeling, Ferdinand J., and Evert H. Van de Waal. "Marginal Information of Maps." *Association of Canadian Map Libraries Bulletin* 24 (March 1977): 5–12.

Paullin, Charles Oscar. *Atlas of the Historical Geography of the United States.* Edited by John K. Wright. Carnegie Institution of Washington Publication no. 401. Washington: Carnegie Institution of Washington; New York: American Geographical Society, 1932.

Rand McNally Commercial Atlas and Marketing Guide. Chicago: Rand McNally, 1876– .

Robinson, Arthur H. *Elements of Cartography.* 5th ed. New York: Wiley and Sons, 1984.

Robinson, Arthur H., and Barbara Bartz Petchenik. *The Nature of Maps: Essays Toward Understanding Maps and Mapping.* Chicago: University of Chicago Press, 1976.

Sanborn Map Company. *Fire Insurance Maps in the Library of Congress: Plans of North American Cities and Towns Produced by the Sanborn Map Company.* Compiled by the Reference and Bibliography Section, Geography and Map Division, Library of Congress. Washington: Government Printing Office, 1981.

Schwartz, Seymour I., and Ralph E. Ehrenberg. *The Mapping of America.* New York: Abrams, 1980.

Seavey, Charles A. "Maps and Documents/ Documents as Maps." *Geography and Map Division Bulletin* 112 (June 1978): 2–18.

Spellman, Lawrence E. "The Value of Maps as Reference Tools." In *Map Librarianship: Readings,* edited by Roman Drazniowsky, 198–203. Metuchen, NJ: Scarecrow Press, 1975.

Statesman's Year-Book. London: Macmillan; New York: St. Martin's Press, 1864– .

Stephenson, Richard W., and Mary Galneder. "Anglo-American State and Provincial Thematic Atlases: A Survey and Bibliography." *Canadian Cartographer* 6 (June 1969): 15–45.

Stephenson, Richard W., comp. *Land Ownership Maps: A Checklist of Nineteenth-Century United States County Maps in the Library of Congress.* Washington: Geography and Map Division, Library of Congress, 1967.

Strickland, Muriel. "The Non-Professional Map-User." *Geography and Map Division Bulletin* 129 (September 1982): 5–9.

Thompson, Morris M. *Maps for America: Cartographic Products of the U.S. Geological Survey and Others.* Reston, VA: U.S. Geological Survey, 1979; distributed by Government Printing Office.

Thrower, Norman J. W. *Maps and Man: An Examination of Cartography in Relation to Culture and Civilization.* Englewood Cliffs, NJ: Prentice-Hall, 1972.

Touristische Veröffentlichungen: Landkarten, Reiseführer, Pläne, Atlanten, Globen aus aller Welt. Vol. 1, *Geo-Katalog.* München: Geo-Center Verlagsbetrieb, 1972– .

Tyner, Judith A. "Persuasive Geography." *Journal of Geography* 81 (July–August 1982): 140–44.

U.S. Library of Congress. Map Division. *A List of Geographical Atlases in the Library of Congress, with Bibliographical Notes.* 8 vols. Washington: Government Printing Office, 1909–74. Vols. 1–4 reprinted by Theatrum Orbis Terrarum, 1970.

———. *United States Atlases: A List of National, State, County, City,*

and Regional Atlases in the Library of Congress. Washington: Government Printing Office, 1950.
U.S. National Archives. *Guide to Cartographic Records in the National Archives.* Washington: Government Printing Office, 1971.
Winch, Kenneth L. *International Maps and Atlases in Print.* 2d ed. London and New York: Bowker, 1976.

Bibliography for *12. Historical Site Documentation—A Case Study*

PRIMARY SOURCES

The following primary sources are all in the collection of the Whitney Library of the New Haven Colony Historical Society, New Haven, Connecticut.

Blake, Henry Taylor. Papers, 1852–1934.
Dana, Arnold Guyot. New Haven Old and New, 1641–1947. (A 152-volume collection of scrapbooks and maps.)
East Rock Park Commission. Minutes, 1880–1889. New Haven City and County Documents, 1639–1899.
Farnam Family Papers, 1872–1935. Family Miscellany, A–Z.
Greater New Haven Chamber of Commerce. Records, 1794–
Mitchell, Donald Grant. Papers, 1881–1892.
New Haven, Department of Parks, Recreation and Trees. Records, 1900–
———. Soldiers' and Sailors' Monument Committee. Records, 1881–1894.

SECONDARY SOURCES

Dictionary of American Biography. New York: Scribner, 1928–
East Rock Neighborhood Association. *East Rock Park.* New Haven: East Rock Neighborhood Association, 1972.
———. *Exploring East Rock Park.* New Haven: East Rock Neighborhood Association, 1974.

Ernst, Margaret M. *"Donald Grant Mitchell and the Birth of the New Haven Parks System."* New Haven: 1980. Unpublished typescript.
First Light Battery of the 6th, 7th and 10th Connecticut Volunteers Monument Association. *Program of Exercises at the Dedication of a Soldiers Monument.* . . . New Haven: Price, Lee & Adkins, 1905.
Mitchell, Donald Grant. *A Report to the Commissioners on Lay-out of East Rock Park.* New Haven: Punderson, 1882.
New Haven. *Municipal Yearbook.* New Haven: Tuttle, Morehouse & Taylor, 1860–1952.
———. *Official Program of Exercises Incident to the Dedication.* . . . New Haven: Judson, 1887.
———. Civic Improvement Committee. *Report . . . Cass Gilbert, Architect, Frederick Law Olmsted, Landscape Architect, to the New Haven Civic Improvement Committee.* New Haven: Tuttle, Morehouse & Taylor, 1910.
———. Parks Department. *Annual Report of the Commissioners of Public Parks.* New Haven: Tuttle, Morehouse & Taylor, 1890.
———. Soldiers' and Sailors' Monument Committee. *The Dedication: An Illustrated Souvenir Program.* . . . Providence, RI: Reid, 1887.
Osterweis, Rollin G. *Three Centuries of New Haven, 1638–1938.* New Haven: Yale University Press, 1953.
Ranson, David F. "The East Rock Soldiers and Sailors Monument." *Connecticut Historical Society Bulletin* 46 (April 1981): 45–60.
Reynolds, Vincent M. *History of New Haven Parks, 1880–1960.* New Haven: New Haven Park Commission, 1961.
The Soldiers' Monument, City of New Haven, Connecticut. Springfield, MA: Miller, 1887.

Notes to *14. The Preservation of Archival Materials*

1. National Research Council, *Preservation of Historical Records* (Washington: National Academy Press, 1986), 5.
2. Mary Linn Ritzenthaler, *Archives and Manuscripts: Conserva-*

tion; A Manual on Physical Care and Management (Chicago: Society of American Archivists, 1983), 47.

3. American Council of Learned Societies, Social Science Research Council, and Council on Library Resources. Committee on the Records of Government, *Report* (Washington: 1985), 99.

4. Relative humidity is the amount of water in a given volume of air relative to the maximum amount of water (as vapor) air can hold at a given temperature, and is expressed as a percentage of that maximum.

5. Garry Thomson, *The Museum Environment* (London: Butterworth [1986]), 68.

6. Paul N. Banks, "Environmental Standards for Storage of Books and Manuscripts," *Library Journal* 99 (February 1, 1974): 341.

7. E. E. Hughes and R. Myers, *Measurement of the Concentration of Sulphur Dioxide, Nitrogen Oxides, and Ozone in the National Archives Building* (Washington: National Bureau of Standards, 1983), 4.

8. National Research Council, *Preservation of Historical Records*, 2.

INDEX